Smiling at Shadows

In writing this book Junee Waites has provided us with an honest and perceptive account of the challenges and joys faced by families with an autistic child—we are taken on a journey with Dane from his birth to adulthood. This book guides us to view autistic children in terms of their strengths and to avoid placing limits upon what they can achieve. The material covered in this book is insightful, practical, and relevant to all parents with an autistic child. I believe that Dane has achieved great successes in life because he and his parents have honored his feelings, strengths, and dreams. I highly recommend *Smiling at Shadows* to anyone who is committed to treating autistic children as individuals and helping them to achieve their personal best—whatever that might be.

Vick Bitsika, Clinical Assistant Professor
Institute of Health Sciences, Bond University

Written with compelling honesty, *Smiling at Shadows* is an engrossing read. It is impossible not to become part of the anguish of parents forced to acknowledge autism in their only child; to be inspired by their dedication and determination to teach him life-skills; to celebrate with them at his "coming-of-age" in an atmosphere of joy, loving acceptance and neverending hope.

A story that will remain in my mind and my heart for a long time.

Dr. Patricia Gaut

Smiling at
Shadows

*A Mother's
Journey Raising
an Autistic Child*

Junee Waites & Helen Swinbourne

Introduction by **Lorna Wing, M.D.**

Ulysses Press

Published by: **Ulysses Press**
P.O. Box 3440
Berkeley, CA 94703
www.ulyssespress.com

Library of Congress Control Number 2002105372
ISBN 1-56975-323-7

First published by HarperCollinsPublishers in Australia in 2001.
This edition published by arrangement with HarperCollinsPublishers Pty Limited.

Printed in Canada by Transcontinental Printing

10 9 8 7 6 5 4 3 2 1

Front cover photograph by Neal and Molly Jansen/SuperStock
Spine photograph by Michelle Wilson
Interior design by Russell Jeffery, HarperCollins Design Studio
Cover design by Leslie Henriques and Sarah Levin

Distributed in the U.S.A. by Publishers Group West
and in Canada by Raincoast Books

This book is dedicated to
Rod Waites

Peace I bequeath to you
my own peace I give you
a peace the world cannot give,
this is my gift to you.

John 14: 27

Contents

Foreword

AUTISM, six letters that seek to describe the indescribable, the extraordinary and complex condition that affects our son, and many other sons and daughters in families the world over. The Waites family is one such family—but with a difference. For the Waites, with the help of Helen Swinbourne, have recorded their personal experiences to share with others and to further open up the world of autism at a time when the incidence of autism spectrum disorder (ASD) is growing at an increasingly alarming rate.

Smiling at Shadows is the story of Junee, Rod and Dane Waites. It details their twenty-five-year journey from the first moments of Dane's life, through childhood and adolescence and ultimately to his blossoming as a talented and caring adult, with a valued place in the community. It is also the story of two parents who, through endless patience and perseverance, fight to insure that their son has every opportunity to live life to the fullest.

However, be warned, it is not the story of a "miracle cure" for autism, as so many books purport to be. It is simply an honest and inspirational account of what is possible with the right people and resources, and with faith in God.

As parents, we found it a very easy story to read. A practical book, that both reminded us of where our journey had started and alerted us to the potential danger signs ahead for our own young son.

At one of the earliest seminars we attended on autism we were told that every person with autism spectrum disorder has a unique profile and set of characteristics. Over time we have learned this to be true as we have worked our way through the early intervention classes and the various educational and therapy groups that have become a part of our lives.

For many, the most obvious feature of autism will be a serious delay or even a lack of ability to communicate verbally. For others, it may primarily be behavioral responses that are cause for concern. Where one person with ASD may exhibit significant motor deficits, another may be extremely agile and athletic. Some children will show an early interest and ability in math and science, others in music, and others will struggle with all academic pursuits. In truth, there is no stereotype of autistic characteristics that fit the frame neatly; there is simply a cluster of attributes that somehow link together in sufficient numbers to warrant a diagnosis of ASD. Perhaps this is why autism is one of the most difficult conditions for the community to understand, for the professionals to treat and for parents to explain.

Despite these differences in autistic profiles, there is much about Dane's life that will hit an emotional chord with families and friends of people "on the spectrum." Reading about his life has touched us deeply. We remembered our own doubts emerging as to whether the behavior of our much-loved little baby was really "normal," but of course everyone assured us that it was. As we read about Dane's special interests we found that there were many that our son shared, straight lines and black paintings to name two. We understand the special joy that nature brings to a child with acute sensory feelings, the rustle of leaves, the freedom of running in a forest, the gentle flow of a stream. Along with Junee and Rod, we held our breath as Dane spent his first night away from his home and his parents—a challenge we also had to face. And sadly, we truly empathized with some of the Waites' experiences with medical and paramedical staff when they failed to understand just how terrifying something like a hospital can be for a child with special needs.

Smiling at Shadows is a remarkable book. It is an insightful and honest account of the often difficult path to adulthood that a child who is "on the spectrum" must face. As such, it is a valuable resource for parents, for therapists, for educationalists and for those in the medical profession. But most importantly, for the general community, it reveals something of the heartache and the joy that comes from living with autism. We sincerely hope that it is read widely.

Judy Brewer Fischer and Tim Fischer

Introduction

It is a great pleasure for me to introduce the American edition of Junee Waites' book, *Smiling at Shadows*. This is the story of her son Dane, who was born with autism, a developmental disorder that isolated him during infancy and childhood from emotional interaction with his parents and other people. It tells how he, in painfully slow fashion, learned to relate to others in his own unique way.

I have a special interest in this story because Junee and her husband Rod first realized that Dane had autism upon reading my book, *Autistic Children*, when he was around four and a half years old. Although the disorder had been present in typical form, professional workers had not recognized it. I am happy that my book was helpful but sad that the diagnosis came in this chance way.

Smiling at Shadows is a perfect title, resonating on several levels. It refers to an aspect of Dane's early behavior as well as to Junee and Rod's courage and positive attitude to all the problems they encountered. Reading this book was a remarkable experience for me, the mother of a daughter, now long grown up, who has autism. Page after page, Junee's descriptions of events in Dane's childhood and adolescence brought back the past in vivid detail. She so aptly conveyed the pain, bewilderment and unjustified self-blame that comes from trying yet failing to interact with a child who has no interest in or understanding other people—who, in other words, lacks innate social instincts. She also beautifully articulated the intensity of pleasure induced by any small sign of progress, often something that a parent of a typically developing child would take for granted. All parents of children with autistic spectrum disorders will empathize with this rollercoaster of alternating despair and hope.

In addition to having direct personal experience with the difficulties and unexpected joys of living with autism, I am also a professional in the field. Over the years I have listened to hundreds of developmental histories of children and adults with autistic spectrum disorders. Although they are exhibited differently by each individual, the same kinds of problems emerge over and over again. The art of diagnosis is to recognize the underlying unity behind the wide range of life stories.

Dane's story is absorbing in its own right. However, with Junee's clear and accurate descriptions of Dane's strange reactions to many everyday events, it is also a valuable source of information on autistic spectrum disorders for both parents and professionals. Through her observations and through comments made years later by Dane, the reasons for his behavior are made easier to understand.

Junee's anecdotes provide insight into the way people with autistic disorders view the world. There are many examples of this, but two in particular stand out in my mind. One is the incident when Junee and Rod were looking for Dane and calling loudly for him. Dane heard them but did not reply because, as he said later, "I knew where I was." This conveys better than any lengthy explanation the inability of people with autism to comprehend the feelings of others, or to understand the actual purpose of speech and communication.

The other story concerns Dane's tremendous fear, as a small child, of the valley road with cows and horses dotting the steep hills on either side. Years later he explained that he was afraid the cows and horses would fall off the slopes. This underlines the difficulty people with autism have in deciphering the information constantly coming in through their senses—a task that presents no problems to a typically developing child. The autistic world is startling in its strangeness but also in its simplicity and logic when seen from the autistic point of view.

Most important of all, Junee describes how she and Rod, along with the many other people who have helped Dane through life so far, learned to deal with each problem as it arose. The exact methods were specific to Dane and his circumstances but the general principles for each example are apparent and applicable to any person with autism.

Prior to Dane's diagnosis, some professional workers tried to blame Junee for his unusual behavior. This book emphasizes one vital lesson: that it is essential to work slowly and patiently with the child or adult concerned, making use of his interests, however atypical, and any skills he possesses. Trying to change him into a different person does not work; he must be loved and respected for himself.

Dane had a good level of ability that was hidden by his autism when he was a child. This underlying ability, together with the love, dedication and determination of his parents and aid from the professionals who did understand, ensured his progress. He still has autism but is coping with the world. After a period of depression in his adolescence, he is now happier and much more settled, enjoying activities with peers who understand and accept him.

The outcome for children with autism in general is variable; some make much progress while others make little, even when given all the help that is available. However, this book has valuable lessons for the parents of all those children, whether mildly or severely affected, who inhabit the strange world of autism.

Lorna Wing, M.D.
Consultant Psychiatrist to the
British National Autistic Society

Just walk away

Rod and I enjoyed my pregnancy. In fact I positively "glowed," as the saying goes. We had been married for twelve happy years and were more than ready to welcome a baby into our lives. I collected a wardrobe of baby clothes, I shopped for all those things babies seem to need, and together Rod and I decorated the nursery. Its cheerful, sunny atmosphere was a reflection of our happiness.

It was very important to me that our children never doubt our love for them. It's not that I felt I was unloved during my own childhood, but I don't recall a sense of being special. As my due date approached, I tidied the house, stocked the pantry shelves and prepared meals for the freezer. I felt that if I were well organized, I'd have time to enjoy our new baby.

Rod and I left for the hospital before daylight. I paused on our front steps and touched the rough brick wall for reassurance. Goodbye house! Back soon—and we'll be a real family.

Two agonizing days and nights of labor passed, the moment of delivery being lost in an onslaught of pain. I had no sense of ecstasy; I only remember the relief in Rod's voice as he greeted our healthy son. Then I became aware of sutures—one after another after another. The indignity seemed endless. When I asked the doctor how many stitches I needed, the reply was a sympathetic grunt: "It's better you don't know."

At last, I could take my son in my arms. I felt a surge of gratitude that he had been able to struggle bravely through such a difficult birth. Then I was overcome with sorrow when I saw the bruising and indentation from the forceps on the left side of his head. Already the swelling had closed his left eye. At that moment my love for this innocent infant surpassed anything I had felt for any other human being. My pain became secondary to his needs.

My son arrived home in a hospital gown to a beautiful wardrobe he had already outgrown. Everything else, though, was in order to cope with a new baby, or so I thought. My well-laid plans collapsed in a heap the moment I arrived home with Dane. Excessive bleeding and intense post-natal pain turned the most trivial task into a massive challenge. I could only grab for the nearest item as I struggled to sit, walk and lift Dane out of his bassinette. However, I was absolutely determined to enjoy this precious homecoming, so decided to set aside my high expectations. After all, it was Junee the super secretary who had set these impossible standards, not Junee the new mother.

Dane was absolutely silent for three weeks. Not once did he cry, or even whimper. Then he developed what the doctor called colic, and began to cry loudly. I demand-fed him every few hours. This gave him some relief, but the crying continued.

The doctor examined Dane again. "He's just a big hungry baby," he said. "It's your wife who needs support. She's exhausted!"

Rod and I accepted the doctor's words without question. I was exhausted, but so was Rod. He was finding his feet in a new job and doing his utmost to help me. In the end, we just existed from one moment to the next.

Then, one day, Dane's cries turned into prolonged, ear-splitting screams that began each afternoon and didn't ease until late evening. When we tried to comfort him by nursing him, he would struggle to push himself away. The health center staff told me that most babies like to be firmly wrapped, but even as a newborn infant he pushed and kicked with amazing strength as I struggled to follow their directions. He seemed to prefer being left alone.

In desperation I bought a *meh-tai*, a cloth sling that held Dane against my body while leaving his legs and arms free. He seemed to like this and my constant movement appeared to ease his discomfort. Similarly, he didn't protest when Rod carried him under his arm like a loaf of bread.

No matter how we tried, we could not interest Dane in toys. His soft toys and bright nursery motifs were lost on him, and even toys that dangled, bounced and squeaked failed to amuse him. Occasionally he noticed his mobiles, but that was all. We could not capture his interest in other ways either. When I tried to look into his eyes, he averted his gaze. Over and over again I would move into his line of vision, and every time he would refuse to look at me, or anyone else.

Imagine, then, how my heart soared when I saw Dane's first smile. For no apparent reason his little face suddenly lit up with joy as I removed his diaper on the changing table.

He seemed to be looking over my shoulder, so I turned around—there was no one else in the room. His eyes appeared to be following a moving object, but he was gazing at a blank wall. I clapped my hands; he didn't respond. Still smiling, he continued gazing over my shoulder at that blank wall. I turned toward the wall again, desperate to work out what he was looking at.

And then I saw the shadows. A gentle breeze was rustling the leaves in the trees outside the nursery window, and this was creating moving shadows on the wall. I found myself crying. I couldn't explain my tears. I didn't want to believe what I'd seen.

Later I opened Dane's baby diary to record his first smile. The little book asked two simple questions: when did baby smile, and to whom? I answered the first question and tried to ignore the second. How could I admit that my baby smiled at shadows and not at me? Hurt and confused, I slammed the book into a drawer.

Dane found such pleasure in the movement of leaves, that I began to place him under a tree in his covered bassinette. While the leaves moved, his screams diminished. I dreaded calm days. In desperation I would swing a branch from side to side to disturb its leaves, hoping the neighbors wouldn't see my unusual behavior. I began to wonder why on some days Dane would be calm for an hour or so while on others for a shorter time. Had he found something else that appealed to him? Eventually I realized he was watching clouds moving across the sky.

Summer's still, cloudless days became a nightmare until I discovered that the motion of his stroller also helped to calm him. When his screams began I would push him around the neighborhood for hours and hours, through all kinds of weather. I couldn't stop to admire a garden or speak to someone because a moment's pause would result in yet another outburst of screams.

I would walk until Rod arrived home from work. While I prepared dinner, he would pace the floor with Dane under his arm. The screams calmed only while Rod walked . . . and walked, and walked. Then we'd take turns eating. One of us had to keep moving until Dane fell asleep. Sometimes this didn't happen until around midnight.

"This was not how I envisioned fatherhood," Rod would say later. "The workload was relentless."

By now Rod and I were beginning to doubt our parenting skills. Although Dane appeared to have no hunger or thirst and I therefore breastfed him according to how I perceived his needs, he was thriving physically. But his emotional needs and wants were a mystery to us. We could only support each other. We would reassure ourselves that all babies go through "stages" and hope that Dane would soon move out of this particularly trying one.

Rod devised a solution for our weekends. Having established contracts all over Victoria for his engineering company, he needed to visit these building sites regularly. Why not combine business with a change of scenery for me? Before long, each Friday night, he'd load up a company truck and we'd all hit the highway. I was apprehensive about our first trip to Wodonga, a town about 180 miles from our home in Melbourne, but Dane seemed to enjoy the rocking of the truck. The deafening din of vibrating steel didn't bother him at all! After three hours on the road with no screams, we rattled into a motel and paced the floor until Dane fell asleep.

The next day Rod worked on the building site while I pushed the stroller up and down Wodonga's streets and around a nearby lake. At lunchtime, Rod bought sandwiches and drove around the town until he found us. He pushed the stroller while I ate my sandwich.

Rod and I explored many country towns this way. A visit to Echuca on the Murray River, where the old paddle steamers are moored, revived happy memories of the time I had spent on a steamer with my parents. They had worked transporting red-gum timber to the sawmills and back-loading general supplies to timber cutters and small settlements. In late autumn, when the water level was too low for navigation, we'd move to an encampment of tents on a sweeping sandbank. I remembered my mother carrying me over the sand to swing in a rubber tire hanging from a tree. I remembered soaking rabbit droppings and squishing the mess through my fingers to make mud pies in the absence of mud. My mother had died when I was twelve, and I found myself listening for the sound of her voice in the gentle murmuring of the river.

The sounds of the river comforted me, helping me to feel less aware of the sense of isolation that our concerns about Dane engendered. Rod's parents loved Dane but they could not accept that there was a problem with their little grandson. This meant that Rod and I were denied the support from them that we'd have otherwise received—support we desperately needed. Yet, how could we make Rod's parents, and his two sisters, understand the problem when we didn't even understand it ourselves?

Of all my friends, only one, Toni, dared ask, "How's Dane?" during these difficult early months. Hearing his screams when she phoned, and knowing I was absolutely frazzled, she would say, "Get yourself organized and drive up here to me. Now!"

"Here" was the fashion store where Toni was the assistant manager. Despite having to serve customers, she still managed to offer me lunch, push the stroller and talk to me about Dane. Apart from Rod, there was no one else who understood, or encouraged, or supported me.

Dane's first tooth broke through at seven months. I knew his bright red cheeks were a normal teething symptom, but I took him for a checkup, just to be sure. I was shocked when the unfamiliar doctor told me that Dane had a red raw throat and infected ears. From the horrified expression on his face, I knew he thought I had neglected my child. He might have been more forgiving had he known that no one could come close to Dane without provoking a screaming session, not even me. How could I know when he was screaming from pain and not something else? But I couldn't explain this to the doctor.

At nine months Dane learned to sit upright. His screaming eased a little, and each day offered snatches of relative peace. With Toni's encouragement, I joined a small group of mothers who had children Dane's age.

It was here that I could see clearly the differences between Dane and other babies. These babies waved and clapped and said "Mum-mum-mum." They played with toys and enjoyed physical contact. They reacted to sound and gurgled excitedly as they crawled toward their mothers. Dane did none of these things, and he had no interest in crawling to me, or to anything else. His smile was spontaneous and engaging, but it was still only directed at shadows on a wall, or leaves moving in the wind, or clouds scudding across the sky.

Fearfully, I began to suspect that I was of no more significance to my son than a table or chair. I pleaded and cajoled for his attention until I felt sick with helpless anger and confusion. Then one day, quite by chance, I lowered my voice and whispered to him. I saw him react to my whisper. His little head moved to one side as if to ask, *Oh, what's she saying?* He didn't look at me, but at least he had responded to my voice. I continued to whisper to him after that and occasionally, and ever so slightly, he would acknowledge the sounds.

At twelve months Dane underwent a routine checkup. I was very concerned about his chronic constipation. We expressed our unease about this, and the screaming, to the pediatrician. Did we have cause for concern? Yes, said the pediatrician, there was a problem. It was me, he said. I was the problem. I was an over-anxious mother.

"Take this mixture, dear," he said. "It will help you settle."

I accepted that the doctor might be correct and became even more anxious. This was my first experience of "blame the mother."

Although he was a year old, Dane had shown no signs of wanting to crawl. Rod and I worried constantly about this and wondered if he'd ever learn to walk, so we encouraged him to balance against a table. Almost immediately he developed a fascination for the straight edges of the table. He would stare along those edges as if transfixed. Soon he became interested in other straight edges. He'd stare along a window ledge, or along the garden fence.

Then, one day, he simply stood up and, balancing himself and straining upward to look along the straight edges, he walked around the table. Rod and I stood mute with astonishment and delight, then hurriedly we moved the chairs aside as Dane walked around and around the table, in a counterclockwise direction. It may have been an unorthodox way to learn to walk, but for the first time he was doing something normal for his age and we were overjoyed.

Following the straight edges of the table became a routine for Dane. I'd see him staring intently at the table so I'd move the chairs and he would follow those four lovely straight lines around and around for an hour or more, always counterclockwise. At last I could keep an eye on him while working in the kitchen.

Dane also developed an interest in the straight wooden balustrade that ran the length of our sundeck—if he wasn't circumnavigating the table he'd walk from one end of that balustrade to the other for an hour or so each day, or until I intervened.

As Dane grew tall enough to see over the table, we tried to play peek-a-boo with him, but he still wouldn't look at us, only at those straight edges. It was as if eye contact caused him physical pain.

Dane also loved to sit near the windows in our dining room. We didn't understand why this was, but at least he was sitting quietly. Then, one Sunday afternoon, he walked straight through the glass door. The sound of the crash was sickening. Terrified, Rod and I rushed into the room expecting to find Dane's mutilated little body lying in a sea of blood. We couldn't believe our eyes. There wasn't a scratch on him. Even the noise hadn't worried him.

Wanting to make sure it wouldn't happen again, I made curtains for each window and attached brightly colored butterfly decals to the glass doors. Later, on a visit to the butterfly house at Melbourne Zoo, Dane became terribly agitated when he saw the thousands of butterflies fluttering above his head. We couldn't understand why, but we retreated very quickly. At home that afternoon, Dane ran straight to our glass doors, touching and carefully examining the butterfly decals. The butterflies at the zoo were moving, of course. Was that why he'd become so agitated?

Dane's fascination with straight edges developed into a strong urge to create his own straight lines. One day, not long after I'd put up the new curtains, I wondered why he'd been in the dining room for so long and went to investigate. I found that he'd managed to pull a thread, shredding those lovely woolen drapes halfway up the wall. He was sitting on the floor beside a bundle of threads, totally absorbed in straightening one thread after another and laying them out in lines.

On other occasions he would attach lengths of string, wool, elastic or any other thread he could find to something secure like a chair or a door handle. He would then pull the thread tight and attach it to something else, pull it tight again and attach it to something else, and so on until all the thread was used up. Then he would admire all the wonderful straight lines he'd created. We called these creations "hang-ups." This obsession remained for many years. Once when he was four and being looked after by a new babysitter, we came home to find our family room filled with a web of yarn tightly stretched from every piece of furniture Dane could find to support his giant horizontal spider web. The babysitter hadn't had the heart to stop him "having fun."

The turning of wheels also fascinated Dane. We would walk with him in the street, each holding a hand as he strained to look at passing traffic. One day he broke away and dashed toward a moving car. As Rod snatched him out of danger, Dane stretched his hand toward those moving wheels, his whole body stiffening in the effort to break free of Rod's grasp. We bought a child-restraint harness and from then on kept a very tight grip on it.

While Dane's non-stop screaming diminished with his ability to sit upright, a multitude of factors—quite beyond our comprehension at first—triggered screaming sessions.

I became aware that certain noises distressed Dane intensely. A baby's crying appeared to upset him most, so I tried to avoid contact with babies. As the months passed, I learned to avoid the sound of trains, and to carefully choose the songs I'd sing to him. Inexplicably, he would tolerate "Frère Jacques" but not "Rock-a-Bye Baby," which made him scream as though in agony.

Nevertheless Dane was a healthy baby, apart from his on-going problems with constipation. He breastfed easily but wouldn't suck a bottle, or a pacifier. The nurse at the health center suggested I introduce solids but he wasn't interested. He'd eat dirt, sand and playdough but we couldn't get purees or cereals into his mouth. In desperation I continued breastfeeding. However, when Dane was fourteen months old, I was told I would have to have a hysterectomy.

I was born with Von Willebrand's disorder, a condition similar to hemophilia, and which had already claimed the life of my mother and three brothers. I hadn't healed after Dane's birth, and was suffering from constant bleeding that had become life-threatening. A hysterectomy offered the only solution. Rod and I had hoped for a larger family but to our immense sorrow, this would now be impossible.

So Dane had to be weaned. Rod took on this task because if I had tried to do it, Dane would have smelled my breast milk and refused the juice. Each morning, Rod climbed out of bed before daybreak, put some orange juice into a small, thick liqueur glass, picked up Dane and then proceeded to walk around the house with him, every now and then dribbling a few drops of juice into his son's mouth. He repeated the process every evening. Dane accepted the juice from the tiny glass but Rod had to keep moving; whenever the momentum ceased, Dane would scream.

This went on for almost four months until suddenly one morning Dane drank all his juice in one go, as if this was the normal thing to do. From that day on he would drink his orange juice without hesitation and I could at least go to the hospital confident that he was receiving some nourishment.

When I came home, Rod and I began eating our meals with one of us holding Dane on our knee. He'd struggle if we tried to cuddle him so we learned to hold him gently and to try to give him a sense of control. At first he'd settle for only a moment or two. Later he'd sit for five minutes or so, then for slightly longer periods. I continued to offer him purees and cereals but, as I made a slow and painful recovery from my hysterectomy, he thrived on orange juice.

One evening Dane picked up a bean from my dinner plate, and examined it closely. So I picked up another bean and placed it in my mouth, trying to encourage him with visual clues. "Put it in your mouth, Dane," I said.

To our astonishment, he put the bean in his mouth and, without chewing, swallowed it! From that instant, he'd eat food from my plate. He wouldn't eat from Rod's plate or a third plate—it was as though the food wasn't safe—but we were so relieved, we didn't care from whose plate he ate.

Apart from Dane's new interest in food, I still couldn't reach him. Over and over again I would tell him I loved him, but he wouldn't respond to my voice. Not once did he indicate that he recognized us. If I tried to make eye contact, he would avert his gaze as he always had. And if he wasn't screaming, he remained absolutely silent.

Finally we found a pediatrician who responded to our concerns. First, he said, he'd need to eliminate the possibility of a brain tumor. A brain tumor! I had no time to deal with my fear before we took Dane to Melbourne's Royal Children's Hospital to undergo a barrage of tests and procedures.

He appeared oblivious to our leaving him in this unfamiliar place. But when we returned the next day, for the first time in his life he appeared to recognize us. As we entered the ward, he almost fell out of bed in his haste to reach us, pointing furiously at a needle puncture mark on the back of his hand. This was extraordinary. Not only was he acknowledging us, he was also pointing to his hand. He had never pointed at anything, ever!

Our hopes soared as we drove home that day. Had the lumbar puncture he'd been given stimulated a vital nerve? Was this the miracle cure? For the first time in twenty-two months we felt alive.

Rod stopped at the local store for bread and milk. He walked back to the car grinning from ear to ear and handed me a newspaper.

"Take a look at this!"

Dane's photograph was on the front page of the Melbourne *Sun,* promoting the Royal Children's Hospital's annual Good Friday fundraising appeal. His angelic little face gazed solemnly from the page straight into my eyes! I burst into tears. Please, God! Why won't my beautiful son look at me this way? Why will he look at a photographer and not at his own mother?

Gently Rod wiped my face. "Hey, Joey, listen to me. Dane wasn't looking at the photographer. He was looking at the camera."

I hardly slept that night. So many thoughts and feelings kept running through my mind—the joy of seeing Dane running toward us and pointing to his hand; my jealousy of some unknown photographer. Over and over I asked myself, had the doctors stumbled on a miracle cure? Would Dane recognize us tomorrow?

He didn't. When we arrived the next day, he completely ignored us. There wasn't even a glimmer of recognition on his face.

Rod and I didn't allow this terrible disappointment to dampen our optimism. We were confident the results of Dane's hospital tests would provide the answers to all our questions. We never doubted for an instant that this baffling mystery would be solved.

The world seemed a brighter place that glorious autumn morning when, with some difficulty, we maneuvered ourselves into a low-slung sofa in the pediatrician's office. As he began to talk to us about Dane's tests, we were dazzled by the bright sunlight pouring through the window and couldn't see the expression on his face.

Physically, he said, Dane was healthy. There was no trace of a brain tumor. An EEG ruled out epilepsy and a series of complicated blood tests eliminated a disorder known as Stokvis disease. He'd shown an elevated level of lead; the reason for this was never explained. Perhaps it was all that walking beside busy roadways. Yes, he *was* intellectually delayed but the pediatrician wouldn't elaborate on this. Rod and I raised the issue of the difficult birth but predictably he wouldn't respond—he was a friend of my obstetrician.

The pediatrician talked without offering any real answers. "The prognosis isn't good," he said. "You're looking at a delayed development that won't go away. The problems will compound and become more obvious."

I can still hear myself begging, "But what can we do? Please, what can we do?"

The doctor straightened a bundle of papers. Then he took a deep breath and said, "You should put your son in the best institution you can find, and get on with your lives. That's my recommendation. Just walk away and forget all about him."

That night we cried with anger and pain. How dare that doctor condemn our son to life imprisonment. For once, Dane sat quietly between us while we sobbed our hearts out. We didn't know where to turn but we knew we couldn't abandon our beloved little boy. We would never "just walk away."

Heaven-sent

As a two-year-old Dane remained totally insular. He smiled at the movement of leaves and clouds and, once, into the lens of a stranger's camera. On some occasions he smiled for reasons we didn't understand. But he still wouldn't smile for his mum or dad, and that almost broke our hearts.

He wasn't curious about anything and appeared to have no need or desire to communicate. Playthings were meaningless to him. He arranged his matchbox cars in straight lines and ignored his teddy bear and cuddly toys. I'd leave cupboard doors wide open but, unlike other toddlers, he never explored them.

Mostly he was silent, but occasionally he would scream with sheer frustration. I guessed when he might be hungry or thirsty and he either accepted the food or drink or shrieked at my intrusion. I never understood why he detested crowds and crying babies.

His obsession with straight lines and "hang-ups" remained strong, but at around two and a half he developed an interest in something else—cardboard boxes.

While Dane's choice of toys seemed most unusual, we were delighted. At last we had something "real" to help him move outside himself into a world of childish play. The bigger the box the happier he seemed to be. Our house became swamped with boxes. He became terribly agitated if I tried to discard a single one.

Around this time Dane learned to climb out of his bed. He would wander around the house at night, and Rod and I worried that he would hurt himself or find his way outdoors. We wondered if we could teach him to associate nighttime with sleep, so we took him into our bed and placed him between us.

I would sing to him, and then I'd whisper, "It's time to lie down, Dane. Dad's eyes are closed. Now Dane, you close your eyes."

To our relief he'd stay quietly between us, rocking his head from side to side, intoning "Aah, aah, aah" till he went to sleep. Apart from his screaming, these lonely, repetitive sounds were his first vocalizations and they were heart wrenching. I ached to comfort him but knew that if I reached out to him I would upset him all over again.

Sleeping between us appeared to offer Dane the security he needed. If he woke and began to climb out of bed, we'd whisper to him that it was still time to keep his eyes closed, and he'd stay with us.

The health center staff said we were doing the wrong thing, but at least we were all getting some rest. So far, we were surviving.

Dane's problem remained undiagnosed. We stumbled from one doctor to another until eventually we received an offer of twice-weekly occupational therapy at the Royal Children's Hospital.

Dane had always seemed to enjoy the car's momentum, so the prospect of the long drives to the hospital and back didn't concern me. Yet right from the start those drives were a nightmare. It was as though Dane was back in the stroller.

He screamed whenever we stopped. At traffic lights, other drivers stared in horror as he shrieked and thrashed about in his childseat.

I worked out a route with fewer traffic lights through semi-rural countryside. He appeared to enjoy this with the exception of one stretch of road that sent him into a frenzy of screaming. There were no traffic lights or stop signs here, and cows grazed peacefully on the hillside. On a visit to the zoo, Dane had shown an interest in large animals, so I couldn't begin to imagine what upset him so much.

At the hospital I had to deal with the problem of sharing an elevator with strangers. If anyone came into an elevator with us, Dane's screams would begin again. So I'd wait for an empty elevator, walk in quickly with Dane and block the path of other passengers with my arms outstretched. I composed a set speech: "Please believe me, it would be better if you let us have this elevator. Would you mind waiting for the next one?" I had to get him to occupational therapy in as calm a state as possible. Our allocated time was one hour and if he started screaming in the elevator, at least half the session was wasted.

While many professionals had said to me, "Don't worry, he's just a bit slow, he'll catch up," the occupational therapist at the Royal Children's Hospital understood that Dane had very real problems. But although she did her best, Dane wouldn't look at her or respond to any of the things in which she tried to interest him. She carried him in her arms. She placed him in a huge playpen and offered him a vast array of toys and sounds and textures. Time and again he pushed her aside as if to say: *Get these things out of my space! Take them away!* With lots of encouragement he eventually played with some large, plastic, interlocking play shapes and circular climb-through cylinders! Of course, like his cardboard boxes, these were *big*!

I don't know if the occupational therapy was worth those nightmare drives. All of our decisions were based on guesswork and intuition, and the therapist couldn't offer specific coping strategies for dealing with Dane's behavior.

For his third birthday, Rod and I bought Dane a tricycle with a little basket on the back. He looked puzzled at first, then he stacked his blocks in the basket and pushed the tricycle around like a wheelbarrow. We tried to teach him to ride it, but he wouldn't. He screamed if we persisted so we had to let him be. The little tricycle remained a wheelbarrow.

Dane needed sturdy, well-fitting shoes for his developing feet so we visited a nearby shoe store. I gripped his leather restraint as I struggled with him to try on various shoes, but he broke away from me, screaming and rampaging through the store. I can still recall the clerk's dismay. We didn't buy shoes that day.

To admit defeat over a simple pair of shoes would have been futile. I asked Rod to look after Dane the following Saturday while I went back to speak to the manager of the shoe store. Not surprisingly, she remembered me. I explained that Dane wasn't being naughty, and that sooner or later he'd need to learn to try on shoes like everybody else. Declining her offer to take shoes home on approval, I asked if she could have a selection of shoes ready for us on Monday. We'd try these quickly, without fastening laces or buckles, then I would remove Dane and collect the shoes later.

The plan worked beautifully. I could see the store manager was pleased too. This was my very first lesson in the art of "preparation." I soon learned not to approach any sales clerk or receptionist without a prior explanation. Once an understanding was established, people were usually helpful. Shopping for Dane became possible, and slightly more tolerable.

Around this time the Royal Children's Hospital ordered a psychological assessment for Dane. Despite me warning the hospital staff that Dane wouldn't respond to a stranger in an unfamiliar environment, he was asked to complete a variety of tests with a total stranger in an unfamiliar room.

After two hours, when Dane had ignored each and every test, the examiner left the room. While she was gone, I suggested to Dane that he help me replace the blocks in their containers and then we'd go home.

One of the tests required Dane to match blocks of differing shapes and sizes with spaces in a container. Without hesitation, he put each and every block into its matching space. As he finished the task I looked up and met the examiner's astonished stare.

"How can he do that?" she asked.

Again I tried to explain that the unfamiliar surroundings, and the manner in which she approached him and presented the task, had created the problem.

She exclaimed, "But that makes a mockery of the whole assessment!"

I couldn't respond. Not only could I scarcely contain my rising anger, I just wanted to get Dane out of that room. I'd promised him we'd go home and that meant right away.

I was delighted when the hospital put me in touch with a playgroup in Croydon. But my pleasure was short-lived. It was at this playgroup that I was painfully confronted with Dane's problems. He was so different. Despite the best efforts of his kind, competent teacher he still wouldn't look at anyone, or sit on a chair or play with toys or with other children. He wanted only to follow the lovely straight line of the perimeter fence. If we dared interrupt, he'd become frustrated and antisocial. I explained to the staff that Dane preferred playthings that were big and "real." His teacher offered him a big bucket of water and a house-painter's brush, and he spent hours carefully "painting" the building's exterior walls.

It was soul-destroying for me to recognize these differences in my son's behavior. And yet his appearance was so normal! I felt so helpless. Did I lack some vital parenting skill? Was I an overanxious mother?

We persevered with this playgroup until his teacher decided it wasn't helping Dane. She arranged for me to meet Joan Groube, director of the Warrawong Day Care Kindergarten in Ringwood East.

As we walked and talked in Warrawong's gardens, Joan Groube described the pleasure she experienced working with a happy and effective team, and how this carried through to the parents and children. Warrawong felt like a happy place to me. The gardens were glorious. There were lawns for running and tumbling, graceful flowering shrubs for playing hide-and-seek, and a host of shady trees. The interior was homely and comfortable. A huge open fireplace, safely screened, dominated the playroom, so the children could experience the joy of warming chilly fingers and toes beside a crackling log fire.

Dane's name was placed on the waiting list, and I drove home feeling that Joan Groube and this wonderful place must have tumbled down from heaven. The thought that our son was to attend what we perceived to be a "normal" kindergarten made Rod and I feel good. It's not pleasant living with the daily awareness that your child is different. The prospect of Dane attending Warrawong, a mainstream kindergarten, helped us to cope with this.

In the weeks before Dane began attending Warrawong, Rod took an overdue vacation and we headed for Lakes Entrance. This was to be the first of many "out-of-season" vacations. It was mid-winter and we knew that with only a scattering of vacationers there'd be no crowds to upset Dane, and few guests for him to disturb.

Despite the occasional outburst, this time with Dane was a joy. He settled easily into a vacation routine. When indoors he'd stand at the motel window, quietly watching passing clouds. Outside, he always wanted to forge ahead, and he'd strain against Rod's grip as they strode along the promenade beside the moored fishing fleet and over a foot-bridge to the sandhills beyond.

We assumed he'd enjoy walking on the beach, but his first sight of the ocean terrified him. We went back the next day but retreated before he became upset, repeating this daily until he grew sufficiently confident to walk beside the surf. Then Rod released his hand and Dane walked on ahead. On one occasion, when the surf grew rough, Rod swept him up, but a huge freak wave welled up, swallowed them both in a swirl of foam and dropped them in a sprawling heap at my feet. They were gasping for breath but otherwise unharmed.

This dumping didn't seem to worry Dane. The next day he walked happily along the beach while Rod and I kept a very watchful eye on the surf. Dane discovered high-water marks on the sand, sufficiently straight to warrant his interest. He ignored the surf and the sand and focused on those lovely straight lines.

Dane began attending the Warrawong Day Care Kinder-garten shortly after his fourth birthday. He cried his heart out each morning—tears of frustration at this change in his routine. The realization that he was crying for his cardboard boxes and not his mother reduced me to tears as well.

One of Dane's teachers, Margaret Whitcombe, was a sister with the Order of St. Joseph of Cluny. In those days she wore the traditional veil. As we left Warrawong on Dane's first day, Rod observed that there probably wouldn't be much love lost between Dane and the nun.

We've laughed often over that remark. How wrong we were. Right from the start Margaret Whitcombe understood Dane's needs. She never worked against his unidentified disability. She accepted the problem and worked with it. She encouraged the children to accept him as Dane, not as a child with problems. This remarkable lady shared our determination to love this silent child who refused to be hugged.

Despite everyone's best efforts, Dane wouldn't socialize at school, always hanging back unless a teacher physically brought him into a group. He welcomed just one little girl into his space. Her name was Jennifer Emery-Smith. She was a very caring child who watched out for him. Dane's lack of speech never bothered her; they communicated beautifully with their own silent, mysterious language.

One day Margaret Whitcombe overheard some children teasing Jennifer about her friendship with Dane. "Dane can't talk! Dane can't talk!" they chanted.

Hands on hips, Jennifer moved to Dane's side. "Dane does talk! Dane just talks when he feels like it!" she retorted. Turning to Dane, she said, "You know our names, don't you Dane?"

Dane, who to our knowledge had never spoken a word in his life, replied, "Yes, I do."

Jennifer didn't bat an eyelid. Still looking squarely at Dane she asked, "You know my name don't you, Dane?"

Dane said, "Jenny." Then, as Jennifer pointed to each child in turn, Dane correctly named each one.

I would love to have heard Dane's first words, but not being there when he spoke them didn't break my heart like that smile he gave for the news photographer. Instead I felt proud and happy that he'd found the courage to take this huge step, and respond to his delightful little friend.

For months after this incident we wondered if Jennifer had some sort of sixth sense that told her that if Dane wanted to speak, then he could. Or had she heard him speak before? We couldn't put these questions to her. She was far too young to be quizzed by anxious adults. Moreover she and Dane continued to operate perfectly well without speech. So we waited, and hoped, but after those few words to Jennifer, Dane retreated into silence.

Rod and I were determined to offer Dane as many childhood experiences as we could. We took him to parks and playgrounds, but he'd ignore the swings and slides and gaze at the trees. Desperately we tried to think of something to expand his interest beyond cardboard boxes and straight lines. When this finally happened, we were almost frightened out of our wits.

One weekend we visited Coal Creek, a reconstructed mining village. Dane viewed the attractions in a vague, disinterested way, with the exception of a lake and a gloomy underground tunnel. I disliked the tunnel's claustrophobic darkness but Dane strained against Rod's grip, seemingly anxious to explore it.

Later, after a moment's inattention on our part, Dane disappeared. Rod and I tried to reassure each other: of course the public wouldn't be allowed into dangerous areas. But Dane wasn't the public! He had no fear of anything and he couldn't read warning signs.

We rushed around the village calling his name. We knew he wouldn't reply, but someone might hear us and notice a child alone. As I ran around the beautiful lake I prayed he wasn't lying on the bottom. Then someone heard our cries. I heard a shout: "If you're looking for a little boy, he's here!"

The voice came from the direction of the tunnel. As Rod and I rushed toward it, a young couple pointed to Dane standing quietly in the gloomy blackness. He appeared to be in a trance, like an eastern mystic in tune with his silent surroundings.

"Why isn't he crying for his mother?" the young couple asked us.

We couldn't answer them. We could only thank them for their kindness.

After Dane's apparent enjoyment of that long black tunnel, I began to wonder about his repeated use of the color black. His first "painting" in kindergarten was a black squiggle. I was thrilled—he was finally doing something that other children did. But the next painting was black, and the next, and the next. For months, Dane brought home one black painting after another. When his teacher removed the black paint and confined him to primary colors, he became terribly upset so the black was restored.

Rod and I gave Dane's first black painting pride of place on his "playroom" wall. Dane didn't exactly "play" in this room; we used it to store his unused toys and now it overflowed with cardboard cartons.

From that first day, Dane screamed if we didn't display each and every painting on the wall of this same room. They had to be in this room; not on the fridge or in Rod's study or anywhere else. As time passed we ran out of space on the first wall, so we cleared a second, a third and then the fourth until eventually the black paintings spread across the ceiling. Whatever could all this blackness be telling me about my son?

The scare at Coal Creek, where we had wondered if our son was lying at the bottom of the lake, made Rod determined to teach Dane to swim. After searching far and wide, he eventually located an indoor heated pool, purposely built for people with disabilities. Here he undertook a special training course in teaching children with special needs to swim.

His first glimpse of the huge pool terrified Dane. The little boy who wouldn't be hugged actually dug his fingers into his dad's neck and held on for dear life as Rod inched his way toward the water. On that first day, Dane didn't even get wet.

Were we trying too hard to make Dane behave like other children? His ability to walk had taken him way beyond leaves and clouds. If he learned to swim, would the squeals and splashing of other children help him relate to play, and to fun? Rod decided to persist.

But it was months before he could get Dane into the water. Every Saturday he would spend two hours at the pool, edging closer and closer to the water, Dane clinging to his neck. Then they'd come home. Eventually Rod's persistence paid off and he could carry Dane across the pool, giving him the feel of moving through the water.

Gradually, Rod was able to hold Dane at arm's length, then turn him around and move him through the water face-first. This went on for more months, and we often wondered if Rod's effort was worthwhile, but he never gave up. Then Dane began to loosen his grip on Rod's arms. Rod would let him bob in the water for a few seconds before grabbing him again. They "bobbed and grabbed" for weeks until one momentous day Dane realized that he could support himself in the water.

From time to time, Rod recorded his thoughts about Dane and their relationship. Of this day, he wrote: "After months of struggling Dane finally became as one with the water. There was no stopping him! The look of incredulity on his face was beautiful. At last I'd been able to give something to my son."

Christmas meant nothing to Dane. He appeared oblivious to our family parties and had no interest in Father Christmas, gifts or decorated trees. So I was puzzled by, though I wasn't about to question, Margaret Whitcombe's insistence that he be included in Warrawong's Christmas pageant.

When Margaret dressed him in a sumptuous recycled altar cloth for his role as a wise king, he responded ever so slightly to the dressing up, and to the rich color and texture of the fabrics. When the pageant began, I could see that for the very first time, aged four and a half, Dane was allowing himself to become part of a group. This was more than his interaction with Jennifer. Now he was coping with the bustle and excitement of the children and the unfamiliar sight of parents and visitors in "his" surroundings.

As the music played, Dane appeared to relax. Then, when the children began to sing, he hummed along with the tune! His eyes brightened and an expression of genuine interest appeared on his face. My hopes soared as it became obvious that Dane was enjoying himself. Then he broke into a radiant smile. He was participating! I blinked through tears of joy.

My joy was short-lived. After raising my hopes at the Christmas pageant, Dane remained insular and without speech. He retreated to leaves, clouds and straight lines, and to his cardboard cartons. Then an embarrassing incident at the National Gallery of Victoria revived our hopes.

Gallery excursions with Dane were difficult but we persisted in the hope he'd notice something. Anything! On this occasion, as we stepped off the escalator at the first floor, he surprised us by walking straight toward a life-size bronze statue of Ceres, naked in all her glory. After examining Ceres from every angle he pushed his index finger into the crease between the buttocks. Then he brought his finger to his nose and sniffed. We could feel a dozen astonished glances: *Look at that little boy trying to stick his finger up the statue's bottom!* We didn't care! He was demonstrating an interest, and he knew where to put his finger to check for an odor.

Very slowly it dawned on us how much Dane hated change, and how quickly he could spot a moved chair, a new cushion cover or a book not quite in its usual position in the bookcase. If I cleaned and dusted his room and didn't put something back exactly where it had been, he would become very upset, screaming and rushing to restore it to its original site.

Rod and I began to realize that Dane regarded visitors in the same way. He disliked the change their very presence introduced. On several occasions I invited his special friend Jennifer to come home with us after kindergarten. Immediately as the three of us stepped inside our gate his attitude toward

Jennifer underwent a dramatic change. He made it quite clear that she wasn't welcome—she belonged at school, not in our home or garden.

Dane became especially agitated and disruptive if friends came by. Sometimes they'd say, "Oh, don't worry, most children don't like sharing their mum" but it wasn't sharing his mum that worried him. This child didn't want to share his house!

Dressing Dane was a taxing, time-consuming experience. He had no idea how to help by raising his arms for a T-shirt or stepping into his pants, nor did he understand that his T-shirt went underneath his sweater, or his socks inside his shoes.

He went to kindergarten for five days each week, five hours each day, though there were times when he became exceptionally difficult, and I would have to pick him up early. Every morning as I left the kindergarten to return home, he would scream. These screams tormented me but I would try to put them out of my mind as I went about my household chores. Rod would always phone mid-morning. We had so little chance to be alone together on weekends or at night that this was a very important time of my day: time to enjoy an uninterrupted conversation, to share ideas and concerns.

Picking up Dane in the afternoon was much easier than dropping him off. The teachers had an excellent communication system: in Dane's bag I would find a note attached to something he had created that day, or describing something special he'd achieved. As we shared a snack I'd talk about these things to Dane, examining his creation or commenting on his achievement. Of course, he didn't reply, but I always spoke as though he understood each and every word.

I began taking Dane for long walks after we'd finished our snack. This seemed to help him unwind, and it quickly became a habit. To avoid any disruptive behavior, I would take him out in all kinds of weather: sunshine or rain, heat or cold. He always strained to forge ahead, so despite his age and size I continued to use a leather child-restraining harness. He seemed to find this less restrictive than my firm grip on his hand. I had to learn to ignore disapproving looks from passers-by.

Autumn was Dane's favorite season for walking. He loved to kick his foot into the thick carpets of dry leaves and watch them scatter. He'd catch sight of a leaf fluttering down from high in a tree and watch its descent to the ground. That's when I'd see his happy face. He'd smile at the leaves. Never at me.

On weekends I tried to divert Dane's attention from cardboard boxes and "hang-ups." To achieve this I needed to occupy almost every moment of his time. After much trial and error, I found I could get his attention with toys like large bouncing balls and giant, multicolored, interlocking climbing-cubes. But the moment I stopped entertaining him with things like this, he'd find something to create a "hang-up," or he'd produce a leaf or a piece of paper to flap from side to side. Gazing at the leaf or paper as though mesmerized, he'd slowly flap it from one side to the other until we'd be forced to intervene. Inevitably a screaming session would ensue. This need for constant attention was incredibly draining.

Maintaining a strict routine—doing the same thing at exactly the same time—usually guaranteed a relatively peaceful conclusion to Dane's day. Evening bathtime appeared to be his favorite time. It was a welcome relief for me too. I'd let him splash water around the walls and onto the floor—the pleasure of seeing his happy face far outweighed the effort of wiping up the spills. I learned that this was a good time to take photographs of Dane.

Dane had been at Warrawong for six months when visiting psychologist, Pat Leevers, handed me a book. "You'd be interested to read this, Junee," she said.

The following Sunday Rod and I spread a rug on our lawn to snatch a few moments together while Dane amused himself walking around the fence, and I opened the borrowed book. Vaguely interested, Rod moved closer and we began to read.

We read page after page, almost forgetting to breathe. Occasionally we'd pause and gasp with astonishment.

Here were our answers! Here was our son, right there in black and white on each and every page of *Autistic Children: A Guide for Parents* by Lorna Wing.

The quiet room

It was as if the author of that borrowed book knew our son. She described Dane's lack of speech, his inability to look into our eyes, his dislike of body contact, his disinterest in rattles and soft toys, and his compulsion for sameness. She spoke of autism as "a pervasive developmental disorder." We didn't quite understand what that meant, but we were to learn soon enough.

I made an urgent appointment with a pediatrician who had examined Dane before. I remember my breathless exclamation as we rushed into his rooms: "Our son is autistic!"

We'd prepared ourselves for a denial, or at least some serious questioning from this man. After all, who were we to diagnose his patient? But after reflecting for a moment, he said, "Yes, I do believe Dane is autistic."

We were speechless. After a long silence Rod asked him how long he'd known this. The pediatrician said that he had recognized Dane's condition some time ago. Aghast, we asked why he hadn't told us.

The pediatrician replied, "Autism isn't a label I'd use lightly. It's a pervasive and life-long disability." We agreed, but his next statement shocked us to the core: "I would not label a child as autistic unless I felt sure the parents were ready to hear this."

This assumption insulted our intelligence and challenged our role as Dane's parents. Forget the prognosis. We weren't fools. We didn't expect our son to be cured but surely doing something—anything—to help him was worth the pain of the diagnosis. We'd struggled and prayed and paid a great deal of money for answers, yet in the few hours we'd spent reading *Autistic Children* we'd already discovered ways to help Dane cope with his autistic world. How dare this man withhold such crucial information from us.

My first reaction to Dane's official diagnosis was relief. I felt grateful that my son's problems weren't the result of poor mothering skills, or inadequate diet or allergies or heaven knows what else. Then the shock hit me. *Why, God? Why Dane? What caused this?* Was it those dreadful forceps at his birth? Was it genetic, or my diet? Rod was angry, asking how could God inflict this on an innocent child.

Then my anger kicked in as I discovered there were many wonderful services available for children with autism. The Irabina Early Intervention Centre for children with an autism spectrum disorder was only a few miles from our front door! Here I learned how critical early intervention is for children with autism. Why didn't you bring him sooner, Mrs. Waites? Why did you delay seeking help? For months, I was overwhelmed with a bitter, burning rage.

Dane had to wait six months for a place at Irabina. In the interim, a teacher from Irabina advised Warrawong's teachers on the needs of children with autism, and coached me at home. She was a wonderful role model for me and as the months passed I began to see the futility of my anger. I needed all my strength to help my son.

Meanwhile Dane developed another interest. He became obsessed with long hair. If he saw a person with long hair, he'd attempt to stroke it and, if possible, he'd try to pull the hair taut into a straight line, stretching it over a chair or attaching it to a nearby object.

He intensely disliked having his own hair cut. Rod and I had always done this ourselves, Rod restraining him as I quickly snipped around the edges. Dane would scream as if we were removing a limb. But Dane's appearance was important to us and we felt that now the time had come to have his hair cut professionally.

I knew this would be traumatic, so I sought out an understanding hairdresser. I explained that the longer we would need to restrain Dane, the more distressed he'd become. She agreed to trim his hair. He didn't react well and left the salon looking somewhat lopsided, but we'd made an encouraging start. With each visit Dane became a little more settled and the hairdresser's task a little easier. I learned to make an early appointment so we wouldn't need to wait, and I'd always shampoo his hair beforehand.

With this little victory on the scoreboard, I decided to give Dane a fifth birthday party—but where? He screamed if visitors came into our home so I looked around for neutral territory. I noticed a smart new fast-food restaurant in town. I spoke to the manager and he promised to welcome any child with special needs.

I was very impressed with this restaurant and couldn't wait to share the good news with Rod. I was enthusing over the smartly dressed young staff with their smiles and good manners, and the securely fenced children's playground when he said, "Where is this place?"

I told him. Then I added, "And, Rod, there's no waiting!"

I was somewhat affronted when he burst out laughing. "Haven't you heard about McDonald's?" he said.

The staff at McDonald's were very helpful and there were no tantrums or screaming at the party. Dane and Jennifer Emery-Smith sat quietly at their own little table next to a window while Dane's young guests feasted and played and rampaged around the playground. Margaret Whitcombe and I hovered in the background, ready to act if necessary.

Dane didn't join in the fun, nor did I expect this to happen. Yet I knew the birthday party was a success. I could see this in Dane's expression as he and Jennifer sat together, Dane silently responding to her reassuring attention. I felt so good about this.

Dane started at the Irabina Early Intervention Centre two days after his fifth birthday. On his first day he traveled home on Irabina's school bus. He appeared calm when I collected him from the supervisor. I wouldn't say he was happy. He'd rarely shown any signs of happiness or sadness, only calmness or agitation. I took his hand and we walked quietly through our front gate and along the garden path.

As we entered the house he suddenly broke into intense, terrifying screams. He kept on screaming and screaming. I couldn't think or speak above the noise. There was nothing I could do to alleviate the frenzied shrieking. Half an hour became an hour, then two hours, then three. Still he screamed. Rod's coming home from work made no difference. Dane just kept on screaming until around 11 p.m. when, exhausted, he fell asleep.

We were stunned. Certain things would still set off his screams—a baby crying, stopping at traffic lights, or while a train passed through a level crossing—but he'd usually settle when the problem was removed or the car started moving. This was completely different from anything we had experienced.

The next morning he was calm as we met the Irabina bus and I handed him to the supervisor without incident. After spending my own day in an unhappy daze, I collected Dane from the bus in the afternoon, and we walked home as we'd done the day before. He appeared calm until we stepped into the house.

Then the screaming began again, screaming that pierced my eardrums and shook my eyes in their sockets. He screamed as if in terror from mid-afternoon until almost midnight. I'm not sure if I cried for Dane or myself or for the pain and confusion on Rod's face. Surely this couldn't happen again? But it did, and the doctor's words from two and a half years ago echoed through my pounding head: *Walk away. Just walk away and forget him.*

Rod suggested we ask Irabina for help. After intense questioning they suggested we use a "safe room" program to help Dane regain control. We were aghast as they explained this extraordinary procedure but agreed to follow their instructions.

We cleared a room of all furnishings and fittings. We placed sealing tape over the light switches and nailed closed the cupboard so he couldn't tear the doors off. It was vital there be nothing in the room with which he could damage himself.

As soon as Dane began to scream, we gently placed him in the safe room. Then we closed the door and waited outside, feeling cruel and helpless. We couldn't leave that door for a moment. The very second his screaming paused, we had been told to open the door, move quickly to his side and offer him a comforting embrace. We had to use the lightest physical contact—he still hated to be hugged. We praised him by saying things like, "Oh, that's wonderful, Dane, you have stopped screaming. That terrible noise was hurting my ears."

Initially he'd start screaming again before we'd even left the safe room. So we'd release him, step outside, close the door and wait for his next pause. Then we'd hurry in again, embrace him and if he didn't scream we'd bring him outside. He'd be quiet for five, maybe ten seconds; then we'd repeat the process over and over and over again until eventually there'd be no more screaming for the day.

Standing outside the door was the key to success. One of us had to provide an instant response to the slightest pause in his screams. To delay for even one second would have ruined the entire exercise. On days when Rod couldn't come home early and Dane was being particularly troublesome, I'd stretch the telephone cord to its limit and call Irabina from outside the safe room. Within minutes a staff member would arrive to support me.

The safe room program was very traumatic for us, but it worked quickly and effectively. Within three weeks Dane's after-school screaming diminished, then stopped. However, he remained very taciturn and needed to be watched constantly. I tried desperately to identify his needs without having a clue what they were. There were certain activities, such as following a straight line or flapping a leaf from side to side, that would keep him occupied for several hours at a time, but to allow him to slide back into his own little world defeated our efforts to involve him in our lives. Often, when I did intrude, he'd become agitated. Then I'd say gently, "Do you need the quiet room, Dane?" and this would calm him.

The "quiet room" episode left me shattered. I didn't expect miracles at Irabina but I was totally unprepared for this sense of helplessness. I'd poured all my physical and emotional strength into coping with Dane. I dearly loved my little son but he gave nothing in return. No smiles, no hugs. No running to Mummy for comfort. Not even a goodnight kiss. Nothing. The faith and hope that kept me afloat for five years was draining away.

My friend Toni changed jobs. I couldn't visit but she phoned regularly and I began to tell barefaced lies. "Yes, Toni, Dane's settling into Irabina and I'm doing interesting things. Yes, I'm fine. Truly!"

I began to develop a fear of leaving the house with Dane. As time went by, I withdrew from everyone and everything. I longed to cover my head and hide in a corner.

Happy faces

Apart from shopping excursions, it was only my part-time job at Warrawong Day Care Kindergarten that forced me to venture outdoors. I began doing the books at Warrawong when Dane was three, and continued working there after he moved to Irabina. It was only here and at Irabina that I felt comfortable discussing my son. In every other situation I found it almost impossible to express my fears and concerns.

At home I directed all my energies into Dane's school programs. I'd constantly employ the techniques I'd learned at Irabina, day and night and every weekend. This was relentless and draining, but I believed that ignoring the techniques for an instant would surely undo weeks or months of hard work.

Establishing eye contact was the first and most important task Irabina set for Dane. Not being able to look at anyone who spoke to him, Dane remained completely disconnected from the world and its people. He couldn't understand, or "see," what it was that we needed to ask or teach or share. Nor could we or his teacher "see" from Dane's perspective. One day his teacher found her teenage son lying on the carpet next to Dane. Both boys were silent and still, and were gazing through glass doors toward a grove of trees.

"What are you doing?" the teacher asked her son.

"I'm trying to see what Dane is seeing," he answered.

Her son's perception amazed the teacher. It changed her approach to working with Dane, and all children with autism. From that moment on she tried to see things through the child's eyes rather than trying to impose her thoughts on the child.

Dane's teacher used music, a loud clap of the hands or snatches of a song to get his attention. To maintain eye contact, she would gently hold his face still until he realized she wanted him to return her gaze. He'd do this briefly, and she'd release her hold.

Although Dane disliked these exercises intensely, we repeated them constantly at home. The moment we did attract his fleeting attention, we'd exclaim, "Oh, that's lovely looking, Dane! Thank you for looking at me!" This was his immediate reward for having glanced at us. Dane needed to believe that eye contact was worthwhile, so we would reward him further: "Now that you've looked at me, Dane, we'll go for a walk." Just a walk in the garden was a very real reward for Dane.

It was twelve months before Dane could look us in the eye without becoming agitated. And we had to continue to work hard to sustain this eye contact. These intensive exercises continued for several years. Then, for many more years, we'd need to remind him with the phrase, "*Looking*, Dane!"

Dane had grown tall now, and his older appearance attracted stronger disapproval when he'd throw a toddler-style tantrum in public. One day, following such an outburst in a supermarket, a shopper tapped me on the shoulder and said, "Give him a sharp smack! That'll fix him."

The intensity of my angry retort surprised me: "I know what my son's problem is. Other than being a busybody, what's your problem?"

I was overwhelmed by incidents like this—added to which was the fear of never knowing when Dane would soil his pants in public. The sheer physical strain of going out became too daunting. As a couple, Rod and I jointly retreated behind our front door. We were so tired of apologizing for Dane's unpredictable behavior, and trying to explain why his needs were different from those of other children. It became easier for us both just to try to support each other.

It was at times such as this in the supermarket that I ached to comfort Dane. This ache became a genuine physical pain. As a smaller child he'd run away screaming if I tried to hug him. By now he'd let me touch him, and put my arms around him, but he wouldn't respond in any way. When I asked for a hug, he'd stand stiffly with his arms by his side, turning his face away from me as he waited for the hug to end.

Just the slightest acknowledgment that Dane understood how much I loved him would have given me so much strength. The slightest gesture from him to me would have worked wonders on my shattered ego. Beneath the veneer of calm I had developed in order to cope I was crumbling, physically and emotionally.

As time went on, I was forced to face the shocking reality that I might lose my temper with my son. I arranged to see Irabina's visiting psychologist. He could see that when I needed help, I would need it within seconds—not in half-an-hour's time or even a few minutes. He understood that I might not even have time to reach for a telephone before losing control.

"You need to find a coping mechanism that is right for you," he said. "You must develop your own coping strategies."

In my search for such a strategy, I attended a seminar where Jean Vanier was speaking. Jean Vanier was responsible for creating the international L'Arche communities for people with disabilities and he sought natural equality for all. I was so impressed with him that I bought his audio tape "From

Indifference to Hope," and here I found words to soften my mood and place me in control of my temper. Jean Vanier taught me to accept my own weakness, and in doing so I became strong. This tape became my coping mechanism. I only had to push a button to create a feeling of inner peace and tranquillity—my own quiet room in the midst of chaos.

And then along came another blessing. Croydon Municipal Council operated a home-care service employing skilled childcare workers, many of whom were specially trained to deal with children with disabilities. One careperson in particular was very special. Her name was Lorna Harman. She had a very calming effect on Dane. She spoke softly and clearly with a precise English accent and this attracted his attention. Not only would he respond to her voice, he also appeared to understand that she really liked him.

Unlike so many other people, Lorna would speak directly *to* him, not around him. She would say, for example, "Dane, is something hurting you to make you scream?" She always treated him as an individual and made it clear that she was his friend.

We welcomed Lorna into our lives. She had the gift of tuning in to any situation and always maintained Irabina's programs with Dane. And she was such fun! She'd join us on Irabina's excursions and, by offering an extra pair of hands, she was as supportive to me as to Dane.

Later Lorna and her husband Derrick began taking Dane to their home overnight. At last Rod and I had a chance to really enjoy each other's company. Ever so fleetingly, we were able to place each other's needs first. On these occasions we sometimes felt, if only briefly, that we were courting again.

Apart from his conversation with his friend Jennifer, Dane remained without speech. It was as if he couldn't move out of the "terrible twos"—that frustrating time just before a toddler develops speech. But now that he was able to look at his teacher when she spoke, he slowly learned to point to what he wanted. At home I used the same techniques as his teacher. I'd take his hand, place it on the cold tap and say, "Do you want a drink of water, Dane?" Then I'd fill a glass with water and offer it to him. The aim was to show him that if he'd point to the tap, the reward would be a drink of water.

After months of painstaking work Dane eventually began to point. Now he could communicate some of his needs to us without screaming.

I found I could briefly attract Dane's attention with a song. "Frère Jacques" was the most effective and it appeared to pacify him. Then he began to sing the words of this song. He noticed songs on the radio and began to sing these too. He'd invent his own lyrics and mimic each instrument. We recognized guitar, drums, saxophone and keyboards in the sounds he made. He introduced each new instrument at exactly the point at which it appeared in the original version. We would have marveled at this talent had he been able to speak.

If Dane could happily sing the words of songs, why, then, couldn't he speak these same words? I raised this with Irabina's visiting speech therapist, Sheila Drummond.

We didn't laugh a lot in those days but we laughed with Sheila. "Junee, how do you feel about singing around the house to get his attention?" She bubbled with enthusiasm. "Yes, Junee! Sing your way through the day! Sing about washing dishes and peeling vegetables and making beds! Sing for Dane to come inside or come for a walk or brush his teeth or drink his milk. Just sing!"

So I sang: "We're sweeping the floor, sweeping the floor! We're making the bed, making the bed! Would you like . . . dah de dah . . . a drink of milk . . . la la la . . . ?"

Sometimes I'd wonder who had the problem, but Sheila's scheme worked. I sang merrily and Dane began to point to what he wanted—and he would look to me.

Until now, each and every experience of dressing and undressing Dane had been an exhausting, exasperating experience. For example, if I asked him to give me his arm, he'd give me a leg. Now, with eye contact, he'd look at me while I spoke, and he'd understand when I'd ask him, in song, to put his hands in the air for a sweater, or raise his foot for a shoe. The dressing process became fun for him. I'd pick up a jumper and sing, "This is Dane's red woolly pullover, red woolly pullover, red woolly pullover. Up with the arms, on with the red woolly pullover!"

Despite the fun, I seriously wondered if Dane would ever learn to dress himself. He was learning to cooperate, but it never occurred to him to add or remove clothing according to changes in the weather. He couldn't express discomfort, so I had to rely on his teachers to find extra clothes in his school pack when it turned cold, or remove unnecessary jumpers on a warm day.

There wasn't much that Dane's teachers could do with a little boy who refused to sit on a chair. So they placed a clock in front of him and if he'd sit still for one minute, they'd reward him by allowing him to stand up and walk around. Then they'd bring him back to the chair. Very, very gradually, his sitting time increased to five minutes, ten minutes, then he'd sit quietly for around twenty minutes while a staff member kept him amused. We repeated the same process at home. After months of patient repetition he could finally sit down and share a meal with us at the table. Now we could teach him some table manners!

Another very important part of Dane's education was developing an awareness of cause and effect. This lesson began with a milk shake. The teacher set out the ingredients and equipment, and then took him through the mixing process step by step. Then she invited him to drink the milk shake. This gave him an understanding that there are stages involved in making a milk shake. I'd reinforce these experiences at home, showing him how we prepared and cooked the various ingredients so that be began to understand that food didn't magically appear at mealtimes.

Dane couldn't recognize happiness or sadness in a person's expression. He was totally unaware that a beaming smile represented a completely different emotion from an angry frown. Rod and I had assumed that recognition of other people's feelings came naturally to all children, and that Dane would develop this skill in due course. It came as a huge shock to us to learn that he would have to be taught to recognize a happy or a sad face.

At first Irabina introduced simple line drawings of a happy face and a sad face. But these were pretend and Dane wasn't impressed. So, in conjunction with his teachers, we collected photographs of adults and children registering a full range of emotions, and straightaway Dane related to the photographs.

As I'd do something that made me happy, I'd make eye contact with Dane. Then I'd point to my smiling face and say, "Oh, Dane, I feel so happy!" Then I'd point to a photograph. "See, Dane, that little girl is happy too." Or, I'd point to my sad face and say, "Oh, I've hurt my finger. That makes me unhappy. This man in the photograph is unhappy too."

We had to exaggerate every emotion to attract even a glimmer of recognition. We needed to act out each change of emotion every day, in private and in public. I'd feel very embarrassed when I walked along a street beaming huge smiles, frowning furiously and making theatrical gestures to an apparently disinterested child.

Dane's ability to identify other people's emotions from their facial expressions emerged in the first weeks of this intensive and long-term program. However, making the connection between his own feelings and expressions was a gradual process.

We used a mirror to help Dane do this. I'd smile at him, point to my face and exclaim, "Happy face! Look at my happy face!" Then I'd draw his head toward mine and together we'd look in a mirror. I'd smile again and say, "Look, Dane. This is my happy face."

Then we moved on to include surprise, fear and anger. I'd explain all my reactions; for example, "Oh Dane, I've dropped my laundry in the mud. This makes me so angry."

Dane had always enjoyed walking among the trees in the park, kicking autumn leaves and watching their color and shapes. Then one day this enjoyment showed on his face. This wasn't just a "learned" happy face—at long last Dane was beginning to express his pleasure.

Dane's Irabina report for that year reflects the progress he made: "Dane shows a sensitivity to feelings, which is quite unusual for children with severe comprehension difficulties and he can both identify and show complex emotions."

For a long time, I had been trying to show Dane how to have fun with toys. Each day I would leave a box of Legos in the same place, playing with it myself when he was present. I tried to show him that I was having fun with the Legos, and that he could too. He'd approach the Legos and arrange the pieces from largest to smallest in a long straight line. Then he'd ignore it until I disturbed his straight lines.

One afternoon he arrived home from Irabina and made straight for the Legos. I watched from a discreet distance as he began to build a tower. To my astonishment I noticed he was beginning his tower with the larger blocks and progressing to the smaller ones. How could he understand this fundamental architectural principle?

Dane's deft touch amazed me as the tower grew as high as he could reach. He wasn't a clumsy child, but until that day I would have said he lacked fine motor skills. For example, he appeared unable to balance his wooden building blocks.

Then, to my added delight, Dane agreed to pose beside his tower for a photograph. This was another first! We'd always had to photograph him unaware, but now he stood impassively while I struggled to steady trembling hands and focus through happy tears.

That photograph of Dane beside his tower captured the very first time I saw him display a pleased and proud response to an achievement of his own. The happy expression shown in the photograph may have been a "learned" happy face, but it left me in no doubt that he was feeling good about his tower.

Building his tower and his response to this achievement was more than just another step for Dane. It was a tremendous breakthrough. Apart from his interest in cardboard boxes, the tower was his first attempt at creative play. In the following weeks he built one tall tower after another.

Then he began using the wooden blocks he'd overlooked since babyhood—apart from arranging them in straight lines, that is. Carefully balancing these blocks, he built a tall shape resembling a space-age building. This wasn't just an up and down tower. This was a real *creation*! Once again he posed for a photograph beside his masterpiece.

Nobody could understand Dane's behavior, let alone Rod. Nevertheless he always tried so hard to involve himself with Dane. Rod saw the block-building as a way to reach his son, to make an emotional connection through the medium of play.

He noticed that one of Dane's blocks roughly echoed the proportions of Melbourne's Osborne Bridge. So he decided to introduce Dane to the concept of bridges, drawing his attention to the Osborne Bridge as we drove past it on our way to the city.

As Rod had hoped, Dane began positioning his bridge-shaped block like a bridge. Rod then fetched a matchbox car and tried to show Dane how he could drive the car over the bridge. No! Dane didn't want to drive over the bridge! He pushed with all his strength against his dad's hand when Rod tried to place the matchbox car on the bridge.

Eventually it dawned on us that while we frequently drove past the Osborne Bridge, we had never actually driven over it. As far as Dane was concerned cars drive past bridges, not over them. So not long afterward we made a point of driving Dane over the Osborne Bridge. After that, Dane allowed Rod to place matchbox cars on his own "bridge."

Rod and I introduced Dane to other bridges. We did this very carefully, not wanting to create another obsession. Dane's teacher encouraged us, reminding us that the student's strength is the initial focus in Irabina's program planning, and is used as a foundation to build upon. An obsession could be harnessed to promote learning.

Dane was still sleeping with Rod and me, but now that he was five we decided he should sleep in his own room. We tried to develop a routine he would accept, repeating the same words each night: "Now it's time for bed, Dane. It's time for you to lie down and close your eyes." Then we'd place him in his bed and as he rocked his head from side to side I'd sing a song and recite a prayer to calm him. Rod and I both slept with one ear open and if we heard movement in the house, we'd get up and gently lead Dane back to his own bed.

One night after months of this routine, we woke during the night to find Dane wandering around the house. To our delight, he responded to my "Now it's time for bed" . . . by taking himself back to bed and going straight to sleep. He slept through the night, and the next night and the one after that. We kept up our vigil for weeks, but not once did he leave his bed until morning. At last we could relax and enjoy an uninterrupted night's sleep. Years would pass, however, before Rod and I finally recognized that once Dane had learned a routine, that same routine was in place for life.

That's a light!

I was very excited. An opportunity had arisen for me to accompany Rod on a business trip to Hong Kong. I desperately needed a vacation, so I was deeply grateful when kind friends offered to care for Dane. These friends were familiar with his Irabina program and we knew he'd be in good hands. Then, early on the day we were to leave, Rod phoned from the office to say he'd just spoken to our friends and that they were now unable to take Dane.

I was inconsolable. Rod suggested I make a cup of tea and he'd phone back. He phoned again, and again, but I couldn't speak to him through my tears. In desperation he phoned Irabina where he spoke to Kath Nicholls, the secretary. Without a moment's hesitation, Kath offered to look after Dane. Kath had worked with children with autism for some time and she understood Dane's programs.

Rod phoned me again. As if from another planet I heard my husband's voice: "Now Junee, I want you to get Dane's things up to Kath Nicholls at Irabina. She's going to look after him for us." I couldn't understand why on earth Kath Nicholls would want Dane's clothes, but Rod was very patient.

In some sort of stupor, I drove to Irabina with Dane's luggage. I felt completely disoriented as I said goodbye to

Kath, and to Dane. I could scarcely comprehend her extraordinary generosity. Somehow I drove home, showered and changed and was ready when Rod arrived home to pick me up.

The satisfying click of the aircraft's seat belt snapped me back into reality. I was on a plane with Rod right there beside me! Oh, dear, kind Kath Nicholls! Thank you so much! Now I could enjoy my excitement as the plane soared skyward. *Champagne, madam? Oh yes, please! Another champagne, madam? Ooh, yes PLEASE!*

Hong Kong was wonderful! I slept late most mornings and then got up and saw the sights. We ate beautiful meals, enjoyed good company, and shopped. My big, lightly packed suitcase was much heavier on the return trip!

Kath Nicholls watched Dane like a hawk while Rod and I were in Hong Kong. But one day, when her husband Geoff was home and Dane was calm, she relaxed a little. However, when she heard Dane's footsteps running briskly around and around the house, she went to investigate. As she stepped outside her door she wondered if a monstrous insect had invaded her garden.

Dane had found a big ball of string. He'd attached this string from shrubs to trees to veranda posts to fences and gates. Every available space in that garden was enmeshed in a giant web.

Geoff observed that Dane hadn't tied one single knot to support his web. He was astonished to learn that Dane couldn't even tie his own shoelaces. Kath said that in her long experience of children with autism she had never, ever seen anything to equal that extraordinary construction.

The subject of knots arose again some weeks later. Several minor procedures were required for Dane's recurring ear, nose and throat problems and he was admitted to a major hospital for surgery. I asked to stay with Dane, but my request was denied. So Rod and I talked to the staff, trying to outline the problems they'd almost certainly confront. We could see the disbelief on their faces as Dane sat quietly on a chair.

We admitted Dane early one morning for preliminary tests and stayed by his bedside until late in the evening. He was quiet and reasonably well behaved, but I wasn't happy about leaving. The following morning, as we stepped out of the elevator, we heard anguished screams. Sick with fear, we rushed along endless corridors toward his room. The sight that greeted us made no sense. Dane lay unmoving, flat on his back in a pristine, smoothly made bed, a pillow tucked neatly under his head. There was no sign of disarray, yet his beet-red face was contorted with rage and frustration. Then Rod groaned "Oh, my God" and ripped the bedclothes aside.

Dane was tied to the bed. His wrists and ankles were bound with strips of cloth knotted tightly to each corner of the metal frame. I had never seen Rod so angry.

The hospital staff hadn't listened to our warnings. They hadn't even tried to phone us when they couldn't control him. When Rod pulled back those bedclothes and I saw my son tied up like some crucifixion victim, I was overwhelmed with rage and sorrow. Furiously we tore the bindings off his wrists and ankles. Rod swept him up and we stormed out of that hospital without saying a word to anyone. The power of speech had deserted us.

Thankfully the operation was successful and our local doctor provided post-operative care for Dane. Rod and I made a promise to each other that Dane would never, ever again be subjected to such horrific treatment.

Dane was still not speaking, and the knowledge that some autistic people never develop comprehensible speech preyed on our minds. Rod and I always talked to him, explaining what we were doing, and why. Irabina's program reinforced our efforts and now his attention was constantly drawn to his surroundings. *Are you thirsty, Dane? Would you like a glass of water from the tap? This is the glass, Dane. This is the tap. See, if you turn the handle, the water comes out of the tap into the glass.* As we said these things, we'd guide his hand toward the object in question.

We named everything we ate at mealtimes. We identified clothing, people, groceries, a passing dog, trees in a paddock and trucks on a highway. From time to time we'd see a flicker of interest.

One evening I lay on our bed reading to Dane. As I finished the story Rod joined us and stretched out with a magazine. Suddenly Dane pointed to our overhead light. Then, in a clear, loud voice, he said, "What's that?"

Rod and I stared at each other in disbelief. Dane had spoken! Then Rod answered, slowly and clearly. "That's a light!"

"That's a light," Dane repeated. Then he pointed to the door. "What's that?" he asked.

Rod replied, "That's a door."

Dane repeated, "That's a door."

Without having given us the slightest indication that speech was on the way, Dane was now asking questions and repeating our answers.

We'd waited six long years for this joyful moment. At first I was afraid to believe what I'd heard. It was as if the image in a treasured family photograph had suddenly sprung to life and spoken to us—such was our initial feeling of unreality.

It wasn't just that he'd spoken—we were also overjoyed that he had spoken to us. We believed that by addressing us directly he was indicating that he valued us.

I have always been thankful that Rod and I were able to share this extraordinary moment. I'll remember forever Rod's smile as he responded to Dane's questions.

For months after that, during every waking moment, Dane would point to things and say, "What's that?" We would answer him and he would repeat our answers exactly, mimicking the inflections in our voice. It was exhausting, but the Irabina staff encouraged me to be patient. It was impossible to predict what Dane would do next.

I enjoyed attending church but the sounds of crying babies still triggered Dane's screams and we'd have to leave immediately. So, with Margaret Whitcombe, we began attending quieter, more formal services in the monasteries and convents. At first we sat at the back, hoping no one would notice us, but Dane would be distracted by the congregation and become unsettled as faces turned to glance at us. Then we took him to the front pew. This was a great success. He appeared at one with his surroundings as the quiet prayers and meditative silences held his attention.

I began to wonder if Dane could be baptized. How should I go about this and which faith should I choose? While Rod's background was Anglican and I'd attended Anglican services and the synagogue, it was our ever-strengthening friendship with Margaret Whitcombe that encouraged us to choose the Roman Catholic faith for Dane.

A Franciscan friar, Father Peter Cantwell, agreed to baptize Dane. We asked Margaret Whitcombe to be his godmother, while Rod's friend Bill Gayfer accepted the role of godfather.

Father Peter created a joyful baptismal day for Dane. He arranged for lots of music and invited Margaret to play her guitar. We had to be careful with the choice of music as some tunes reduced Dane to tears. One song he did appear to enjoy was "Kum By Ya," so it was decided that Margaret would play this during the ceremony.

As Dane recognized the familiar tune he turned his head toward his new godmother. I saw the sheer delight on Margaret's face as he looked into her eyes and began to sing

the words of the song. For the very first time in his young life
Dane had truly connected with another human being.

Not long after the baptism, Dane began to spend weekends with Margaret in the Cluny Convent. Margaret could
see that without the help of an extended family I was approaching physical and emotional exhaustion, so she sought permission from the convent for Dane to stay. While it was not
unusual for a child to visit the convent, letting a youngster
stay overnight was a new and somewhat radical idea. However,
the supportive convent community agreed to give it a try.

It wasn't long before Dane became friends with the
members of the community. Each sister discovered a way to
connect with this little boy whose communication skills were
so limited. In his own way, he responded to these kind people
and their beautiful surroundings. When he met the elderly
Cluny Hostel residents in corridors and the sitting room he
slowly made friends with them too.

Cluny's environment had all the right ingredients for
Dane to feel secure and comfortable. The orderly, structured
life with its routines for meals, prayers and bedtime suited him.
And he was with his beloved godmother who was prepared
to devote all her time and attention to him. Together they did
the things he appeared to enjoy: walking beside the Yarra
River or through parks and gardens, and taking tram rides.

The kindness of Margaret and her community was
such a blessing. At last Rod and I could go to the movies or a
restaurant, or stay home and sleep. When we'd arrive at the
convent to pick Dane up we'd be asked to stay for afternoon
tea. We began to share our joys and sorrows, and discovered
the love and strength of a wonderful new family.

At six years of age, Dane still demanded his own space, reject-
ing any person he didn't know very well. Apart from little Jennifer at Warrawong, he had always avoided other children.

Then dainty, dark-haired little Erin Young, who was also at Irabina, decided she'd be his friend. To our surprise Dane didn't object. Erin was also autistic and, like Dane, enjoyed music and movement. She had speech and didn't object to Dane's persistent questions. She flitted around him incessantly, always using his name. "Come on, Dane," she'd say. "We'll go there, Dane. Is that all right, Dane?" Erin was the organizer.

Dane was beginning to point to identify his needs and his eye contact was slowly improving. For months he continued to ask "what's that" and repeat our answers over and over and over again.

This very early speech was not echolalia—the constant repetition of speech characteristic of people with autism. Rather, these question-and-answer routines reflected his developing interest in his surroundings. Suddenly, however, all this changed as echolalia made its appearance.

Dane began to repeat our questions to him. We'd ask, "Are you thirsty Dane? Would you like a drink? Please say yes or no."

Over and over he'd repeat, "Are you thirsty Dane would you like a drink please say yes or no . . . Are you thirsty Dane would you like a drink please say yes or no." Then he'd become terribly frustrated because he couldn't answer us. It was as though he couldn't formulate "yes" or "no" as an answer to our question.

He would also reproduce the rhythm and inflection of our words. For example, if I said, "*Dane*, you are a *good* boy," he'd endlessly repeat, "*Dane*, you are a *good* boy . . . *Dane*, you are a *good* boy . . . ."

In time he'd repeat more involved sentences—"We'll go for a walk when Daddy gets home . . . we'll go for a walk when Daddy gets home"—but he couldn't ask me to take him for a walk.

Dane's early echolalia could be a real crowd stopper. Sometimes there'd be angry looks from passers-by who assumed he was poking fun at them. I would find myself wishing that just for a moment or two he'd stop talking, and then I'd feel guilty.

A number of children with autism don't go beyond echolalia. Perhaps it feels safe to them. They don't have to learn anything more, or venture into the unknown.

Despite the echolalia, and his lack of toilet training, I felt that Dane was moving ahead. His screaming sessions had diminished, his demeanor had improved, and he was beginning to understand other people's reactions and to develop his own facial expression. And his first school report was mostly positive. He had started at Irabina at five, completely devoid of speech or communication. Now he was six and, as the report said, his language had "improved significantly so that he is able to express his needs and basic feelings, make observations about the activities of others and use monologue to help control his own behavior." The report continued:

> *His attention and concentration can be sustained for 30–40 minutes at early reading, writing, drawing and language activities. He is now able to "sound" three-letter words, has a considerable sight-reading vocabulary and is able to construct simple sentences using word cards. He enjoys parallel play (bike riding, ball activities, block building) with other children and interacts with "rough and tumble" and "fun" games at an approximately three-and-a-half-year level. His comprehension and verbalization of his own feelings have enabled him to feel concern for others, and to share in their enjoyment.*
>
> *Although Dane seeks and enjoys social interactions he seems to comprehend only distinctly positive and negative responses and is confused by any subtleties in social situations. His behavior therefore can be impulsive and unpredictable. He still needs a good*

deal of assistance, and is not yet able to occupy himself
for any length of time.

From time to time Dane was required to undergo comprehensive psychological evaluations to gauge his levels of
functioning. I looked forward to his next evaluation in the
certainty that the consulting psychologist would be delighted
with his progress. Maybe I'd get a pat on the back too!

After the evaluation, the psychologist came to our
home to interview Rod and me. As she spoke, I began to
wonder if she had muddled her paperwork. Were we discussing the same child? She highlighted gaps in Dane's skills and
functioning and pointed out how these lagged a year and
three months behind his chronological age.

"One year and three months?" I said. "Surely that's not
a problem? We can help him catch up!"

But the psychologist shook her head firmly, explaining
that the gap would continue to grow. "You're not seeing the
overall picture. One year and three months will soon become
two years, then three years and so on. He'll only get worse."

I struggled to hold my tongue and contain my welling
agony. I must open my mind to professional opinion. "What
exactly are you trying to say? Let's be absolutely open!"

The psychologist replied, "You must consider placing
Dane in care. You'll have to make this decision sooner or
later. You must consider it now."

I believe this psychologist saw our situation only from
a clinical viewpoint: *This child is a non-performer. He's never*
going to amount to anything. He has no future, so why not
institutionalize him? She wasn't suggesting that other people
might give Dane better care than we could. In fact, she didn't
even ask us whether we wanted to care for our son, or how
we were coping as his parents.

I didn't cry. I couldn't cry. I couldn't even begin to face
my excruciating pain so I tried to ignore it. Rod was angry,

very angry. Never again would "they" evaluate his son. Never again would "they" set foot in our house.

But despite Rod's anger and exasperation with contradictory professional opinions, Dane was obliged to undergo yet another comprehensive assessment. This one used an autism-specific educational profile with the results displayed as a clear, eye-catching pie chart, offering teachers of children with autism an instant and accurate point of reference from which to begin working with each child. The segments of each child's pie chart were shaded from white, representing the highest degree of competency in a specific skill or task, through shades of gray to black, for the lowest levels of competency.

There were no shades of gray on Dane's chart. A solid black circle jumped off the page as if sneering, "This is your son!"

I could not ignore the implications of that ominous black circle. I could no longer take comfort in the euphemism "autistic tendencies." I had to address the painful fact that Dane was classic autistic. This meant that my son faced a lifetime of difficulties with social relationships and verbal and non-verbal communication, that the development of his imagination and ability to play would be delayed, and that any change in his routine would always be strongly resisted. I had to accept the professional advice: *Your low-functioning son will never develop the skills to care for himself.*

This dismal prognosis forced us to address the question of our son's future should either of us die or become incapacitated before Dane's eighteenth birthday. (After his eighteenth birthday a tribunal would make the necessary decisions.) There would be no alternative but for Dane to be placed into care. But where? It was our responsibility to nominate the facility of our choice. After hours of telephoning we made appointments to inspect four highly recommended facilities. I was grateful for Margaret's company as we set off that day.

Nervously we approached the first place through an imposing entrance and up a sweeping driveway. The aroma of freshly brewed coffee restored my spirits as the administrator ushered us into the grand building and made us feel very welcome. We discussed our needs in minute detail and were told, yes, this facility could meet those needs. I think I became mildly euphoric. Even Dane appeared impressed.

The administrator's smile faded slightly when Rod asked if we could inspect the residents' accommodation. An orderly escorted us along a thickly carpeted hallway and paused to unbolt a heavy door.

We couldn't have imagined the indescribable dreariness on the other side of that door. Nothing could have prepared us for the gut-wrenching misery we saw on the faces of the people there. Margaret called me over to a window and pointed to a walled exercise yard. It could have belonged to a prison.

While the staff in the second and third facilities seemed sincere, and anxious to help and reassure us, the accommodation was no better. In sad, stunned silence, we drove to our last appointment, only to find yet another elegant façade.

We all fell into a terrible despair as Rod turned the car toward home. We drove for a while in silence, then Rod pulled off the road. He stepped out of the car and slowly walked across a grassy open space toward a grove of trees. I sensed he didn't want Margaret to see his tears.

Dane stared intently at his father as Rod disappeared into the trees. I was surprised to see an expression of genuine concern on his face. "Daddy sad?" he asked.

I replied, "Yes, Dane, Daddy's sad. He's sad because those people looked so sad."

Dane climbed out of the car and ran toward Rod. Margaret and I held our breath; we'd never seen Dane react in this way. We saw Rod turn and stare. Then he laughed and threw his arms into the air and shouted, "Come *on* son! *Run* to me! *Run!*"

Dane jumped into his father's arms and for a wonderful moment, we watched Rod laughing and crying and hugging his son. Later Rod wrote down his thoughts: "I'd never experienced anything like this before. The despair and degradation of those people overwhelmed me. I had to stop the car and stride off into the bush; I couldn't let my family hear the sobs of grief that racked my insides. Then I heard Dane's running feet and saw his beautiful blue eyes looking up at me as he jumped into my arms. He didn't speak, but this sudden show of affinity pierced my heart. I knew then that if my son could witness my despair and respond to me with such silent strength, I could overcome my own dread and move on."

Rod and I made no decisions that day about where Dane would go if we died or became incapacitated. Instead, we nominated Margaret as his legal guardian so that she would have input into decisions about where he would live.

The cup finishes

Dane's recent Irabina report weighed on my mind. It was the ending that worried me: "Dane's progress is very dependent upon the control and encouragement of the adults in his world." Would I have the strength to give Dane this control and encouragement? Could I maintain Irabina's high standards at home?

With no chance to convalesce I'd been unwell since Dane's birth. Margaret suggested I take a complete rest at a retreat house operated by Franciscan friars. She offered to care for Dane during the week while Rod would take him home for weekends.

I became a temporary resident at La Verna, a silent retreat. I was invited to sleep all day if I wished, or attend Mass and join the discussion groups. The sleeping sounded wonderful and I slept for days and nights! Apart from attending Mass I kept to myself for a while. As my spirits revived I began to realize how utterly exhausted I'd been.

I came to terms with God on that retreat. I discovered answers to that perennial question, "Why me?" Why did my mother die when I was twelve? Why couldn't my foster mother Alice Wuillemin be there for me when I most needed her? I couldn't have found a more loving and supportive extended family when Maxine Wuillemin befriended me at school, so it was a sad coincidence that just when I most needed that family's support with Dane, Alice was coming to terms with the tragedy of her daughter Andrea's multiple sclerosis. Added to this, I felt burdened by my guilt that I couldn't be there for her either.

On the retreat, I read *Five for Sorrow, Ten for Joy* by J. Neville Ward. This writer explained how there's pleasure and sadness in most days but by sharing this with God I could award myself five points for sorrow and ten for joy. He explained how I could really enjoy the good parts of each day and just accept the not-so-good. As I read this book, my God of retribution became a God of love.

I stayed at La Verna for nine days. Unknowingly, I had made a Novena! I left truly understanding the words of Jesus in John 14: 27: "The peace I give to you, the world cannot give."

After Dane's baptism and my La Verna retreat I resolved to receive the Roman Catholic faith. I joined Melbourne's first open, community-based, adult catechumenal group. I felt privileged to be following an ancient tradition just as the Church introduced this new method of welcoming adults into the faith. My confirmation was a culmination of many blessings and I rejoiced in the opportunity to declare my belief that God is alive and present, and allows me to feel loved and to forgive and be forgiven. God is the Alpha and the Omega and the Eucharist is the center of my being. I began to attend Mass at La Verna's chapel with Dane and Margaret.

As Christmas approached, the friars at La Verna asked me if Dane would be part of their annual nativity play. The significance of this touched my heart. St. Francis of Assisi began the tradition of nativity plays in the knowledge that simple village folk would be more likely to understand what they saw rather than the spoken word. St. Francis would have been a wonderful teacher for children with autism.

Dane will always remember what he saw on that beautiful Christmas Eve—the oxen and the hay, the candles and the crib, Mary and Joseph and the baby Jesus. All these visual props helped him to comprehend the meaning of Christmas. I could see the interest in his eyes as he walked in the procession from the chapel to the nativity scene. This comprehension was God's special Christmas gift, to me.

The quiet of a candlelit chapel provided a more acceptable way of calming Dane than his habit of flapping small flexible objects from side to side. This obsession began when he was a toddler and persisted for years.

Always looking into the light, Dane would hold a leaf or a piece of paper at eye level between his thumb and forefinger. Then he'd flap the item from side to side as though to the rhythm of music. He'd become mesmerized, sometimes for an hour or longer, and we'd need to find a very effective distraction before we could intervene.

Rod and I began to offer timed activities as an alternative to the flapping. We'd say, "You can flap your leaf for five minutes, then we'll walk for five minutes, then we'll listen to music for five minutes." We were beginning to recognize how much Dane disliked that feeling, even momentarily, of having nothing to do. The more structure we could build into his day, the calmer he appeared to be. Then we'd ask ourselves if there could be too much structure in his life. We didn't want him programmed like a robot.

As his language developed we'd ask, "Dane, what makes things flap?"

He'd reply, "The wind."

"Are you the wind, Dane?"

"No."

Very firmly, we'd say, "Then don't flap!"

When his flapping became inappropriate, we'd ask, "Dane, are you the wind?" This cue became his control and he'd move to another activity. Dane didn't abandon his flapping and we couldn't force him to. He enjoyed "being the wind." But at least he had this obsession under control.

His obsession with straight lines remained strong. He gazed at stripes on a tablecloth or a beach towel. He walked around a perimeter fence for hours if we let him. Rod and I discovered that if we could sit in the middle of a smallish, fenced paddock where we could keep a watchful eye on Dane walking the boundaries, we could enjoy a picnic, of sorts. We did this so often it's a wonder we weren't arrested for trespassing.

Then he discovered mortar lines in brick and stone walls. He'd lean down or stretch up on his toes to focus on a single line, and away he'd go. Given the opportunity, he'd have followed a line along the length of the Great Wall of China. He'd find a mortar line on a city building and insist on following it, screaming each time I changed direction or crossed a road. I learned to suggest he follow other straight lines in the directions I wanted to go. I avoided eye contact with curious pedestrians. I was painfully aware that my son was doing something completely unacceptable for his size and age. Often I wanted to slide down between a crack in the pavement and become invisible.

Dane became passionate about trees. In the street he would break away from us, run toward a tree and throw his arms around it with a rapturous expression. Parks were happy places. Here, as Dane hugged the trees and ran his fingers over their bark, we could watch our son's beautiful smile. At least he'd smile for the trees, if not for us.

In our garden he would shake the young trees we planted until they broke away in his hands. They coppiced from their stumps and neighbors would ask about our unusual "shrubs."

We'd reply, "Oh, those? They're oak trees."

"Oak trees? Surely not!"

It was Rod's idea to teach Dane to identify trees. Before he'd shaken the living daylights out of one, we'd restrain him and say, "Oh, look at this lovely silver birch." Or, "Look, Dane, this is a poplar tree." The speed at which he learned to identify trees astonished us. Within weeks he could name the trees alongside the roads, in parks and in private gardens, and as he became more proficient we'd locate different varieties in the botanical gardens.

In those days we made countless visits to city specialists. As his reward for good behavior, one hour with the trees in the botanical gardens became infinitely more appealing than ice cream.

It wasn't just the prospect of being with trees that encouraged Dane's good behavior. By carefully explaining our plans for the day, we overcame his fear of not knowing what would happen next. However, we didn't understand this very real terror for years to come.

Recognizing trees provided Dane with his first point of reference for interacting with others. After we replaced our broken oak trees with a plantation of silver birch he began asking complete strangers, "Do you have silver birch trees?"

As an older child he began to relate trees to their country of origin. For example, he learned that maple trees came from Canada, then he learned to find Canada on the map. After that he examined picture books relating to Canada. His curiosity began to develop, but he didn't know how to ask questions outside his own safe topics. For Dane, trees were a very safe topic.

For a week's vacation, we hoped the northeastern Victorian town of Bright—famous for its natural attractions—would appeal to a young man in love with trees.

I must have sounded quite demanding when I phoned to inquire about accommodations. "May we have a very private room overlooking trees? With big windows?"

A motel on the edge of town offered us a suite that overlooked the fast-flowing Ovens River. This was Dane's first experience of a fast-flowing river. It appeared to calm him. It was as though the sounds and movement of the river lulled him into a sense of well-being.

The trees were shedding their autumn color. Dane waded through drifts of leaves and gazed into the river's clean cold water tumbling over smooth stones. Inside our motel suite he'd stand at the window gazing at the water and at the flocks of brightly colored parrots feeding in the grass and swooping from tree to tree.

By now, taking photographs of Dane had become second nature. My first requests, when he was just a toddler, that he smile for Mummy had been met with a blank expression. I learned to appeal to his strong sense of reality and to ask that he smile for the camera. He would immediately respond with a broad grin. He appeared to understand that it wasn't Mummy who produced the photograph, it was the camera. So he must smile for the camera.

It was at Bright that Dane first smiled for me, and not for my camera. He was knee-deep in autumn leaves when he turned and gave me a lovely smile, saying, "Smile for Mummy."

I checked—the camera wasn't in my hand. "Smile for Mummy? Not for the camera?"

He replied, "Yes! Smile for Mummy!"

I had to hide my joyful tears. I didn't want him to think his beautiful smile had made me unhappy.

Then he said something I had longed to hear. "Dane's a happy boy!"

Dane's perceptions—so vastly different from those of other people—still confused us. By now we knew that he heard *everything*. He heard not just the speaker but all those sounds that to us are just a background hum—traffic, birdsong, a distant lawn mower, a barking dog. For Dane every sound is equally important and demands his attention.

His visual perceptions are vastly different too. One morning at Cluny Convent a sister came to breakfast without her veil. Dane tapped his godmother on the arm and said, "Look, Margaret. Catherine's had a haircut."

Dane often stared sideways with a puzzled expression, as if he didn't know what he was looking for. He couldn't discern an individual within a group. It seemed to me that he could see only a frightening jumble of heads and torsos and limbs. Once, at a church bazaar, I asked him to give a package to a lady almost within reach of where we were standing. I knew he recognized the color red, so I pointed out the bright red coat she was wearing. Dane immediately became terribly agitated. I couldn't understand why. Then, away in the distance, I noticed another woman in a red coat. He had simultaneously identified both red coats and become confused.

Nor could he relate stick figures to the human form. I'd suggest he copy my stick figures and he'd draw a rough circle with disconnected straight lines. Similarly he couldn't comprehend or copy my "houses." On his page he'd produce a jumble of windows, doors and roofs.

Rod and I began to understand that whereas we might see, for example, a new house in a paddock, Dane's perception of that same scene would be much more comprehensive than ours. We'd focus on the house. Dane would see the house, the earthworks, the road, the fences, the machinery and the trees— every single minute detail of that scene would demand his attention. And he'd remember every detail as well.

Dane lacked the simple skills other parents take for granted in their children. He couldn't suck a milk shake through a straw or blow out the candles on his birthday cake. I bought a wire ring for blowing bubbles in the bath. He enjoyed the bubbles I blew but had no idea how to do this himself. Irabina introduced balloons in an effort to teach him to suck and to blow. He responded well to the balloons and was soon drinking his milk shakes and blowing out candles with gusto. Rod and I were thrilled. For us the achievement of these simple skills was cause for celebration.

Dane's immense enjoyment of balloons gave us the opportunity to divert him from his obsession with "hang-ups." We did this in stages, and with Irabina's help. First we allowed him to keep a "hang-up" until the following meal-time. Then we insisted the "hang-up" be dismantled. Once he accepted this, we'd allow him to tie a piece of string (representing a "hang-up') onto a balloon, and to hang the balloon inside the house. In no time he became obsessed with balloons!

Now what would we do? We were overwhelmed with balloons so Irabina suggested we confine them to special occasions and vacations. Rod and I promised to have balloons for all our birthdays and anniversaries, and on vacations. At home, we allowed him to leave the balloons in place for one day. Vacations were different—we allowed him to leave his balloons in place for days at a time.

We always kept our promises and he began to identify balloons with special occasions, accepting that they had a time and place. Woe betide me if I forgot to take his balloons on vacation. I vividly remember knocking on a country news-vendor's door moments after closing time and begging the surprised proprietor to please, please sell me some balloons!

Our most memorable "balloon" vacation took place with a horse-drawn gypsy caravan. Dane decorated every nook and cranny of that caravan with balloons and streamers and indeed we looked like a colorful gypsy family! Even

Blackie, the Clydesdale that pulled the caravan, wore streamers on his bridle. Dane loved Blackie, a gentle giant in every sense.

At night we stopped and made camp. We'd give Blackie a good rub-down, then Rod would hoist Dane up onto the big horse's back and lead them through the bush. After our campfire meal we'd lie in our sleeping bags, gazing into the night sky and listening to the crickets and Blackie's gentle snuffling.

Dane hadn't noticed stars before and he was intrigued by them. By the end of that vacation he had memorized everything Rod could tell him about stars, planets and constellations. He'd repeat this information over and over again.

Dane's echolalia had expanded from the constant repetition of other people's questions and answers to the repetition of long and complex conversations. Despite this ability, however, he still couldn't answer any of my questions about his day at school. I tried various approaches without success. He was unable to talk to me about his day at school.

Then he'd step under the shower, and all would be revealed. With the water running, he'd begin "thinking aloud," and as he spoke, I could identify the different voices of his classmates at school. I'd also hear the voices of his teachers. Jokingly, I'd warn them not to discuss anything private within earshot of Dane.

This repetition of other people's speech demonstrated Dane's excellent memory and his remarkable ability to copy, but it didn't help us to communicate with him, or he with us. No matter how carefully we avoided open-ended questions, we'd seldom get more than a "Yes, Mum" or "No, Dad" or "Good." And Dane still couldn't express anything more than his most basic needs. His frustration at this inability continued to trigger bouts of screaming and disruptive behavior. As a family we were having almost no interaction with other people.

Our friends Greer and Llewyn Waters sensed this bad patch and invited us to their farm in the Bega Valley, a day's drive from Melbourne. Dane detested the slightest change in his daily routine and we wondered if we could accept our friends' generous offer. Could Dane possibly cope with a long, long drive?

Rod and I were learning to use coping strategies. We'd learned that before we left home we needed to explain why we were going away, how long we'd be away, and when we'd be coming home. Before the trip to Bright we had shown Dane road maps, explaining exactly how long we'd be on the road and where we'd stop for lunch, and we showed him photographs of the motel.

Remembering Dane's fascination with the Ovens River at Bright, Rod wondered if we could use rivers as a coping strategy for the journey to Bega. So he planned our trip according to the rivers we'd cross. He explained to Dane that we'd have morning coffee at this river, lunch beside that river, and afternoon tea beside yet another river. And in between we'd cross all these other lovely rivers, too! This really appealed to him.

The trip to Bega passed without major incident. And the vacation with our friends restored our health and sanity. We arrived home with spirits revived, and began to think of rivers as our friends. As Dane began to learn their names we became more adventurous, traveling farther afield seeking things to see and to do that would provide him with new experiences.

I had often wondered if Dane was the world's only seven-year-old who wasn't toilet trained. While other children went to school with books and toys, Dane's schoolbag bulged with clean clothes. We knew he disliked sitting on the toilet but it was a long time before we discovered that he was afraid that he'd fall down it and disappear. Reality didn't worry Dane. It was the unknown that scared the wits out of him.

The dead goldfish episode did nothing to alter this perception. Without thinking and with Dane looking on, Rod flushed a deceased pet fish down the toilet. This convinced Dane that anything that didn't put up a jolly good struggle should follow the dead fish. We soon developed an intimacy with the local plumber. "You're not having the septic pumped out again!" astonished neighbors would gasp.

We couldn't even begin Dane's toilet training until he learned to look at us, and until we could hold his attention. Then we began using rewards. If he sat on the toilet seat for a few seconds we'd give him a lollipop or a sip of lemonade. Slowly we extended this time, and when he finally stayed on the seat for a minute or so we replaced the rewards with verbal encouragement: *Oh, what a clever boy, sitting there so calm and still!*

I'd leave the toilet door open when I went and say, "Dane, I'm going to sit on the toilet now." Usually he ignored me. Very occasionally he'd nod approvingly. After he developed speech he'd sometimes say, "Good Mummy! Oh, good Mummy! Lollipop or lemonade?"

I began to show him what happened while I was on the toilet: *Isn't it nice to have clean underpants. See, Dane, I don't have soiled pants.* I tried to attract his attention as I scraped the contents of his soiled pants into the toilet: *See, Dane, this is where it goes.*

His teachers at Irabina used the same techniques, but we appeared to be getting nowhere. I began to have visions of an adult son in protective clothing.

Then one morning Rod hurried up to me whispering, "I think Dane is sitting on the toilet!"

We waited, eventually hearing sounds that were music to our ears: the sound of paper being torn from the roll, of the bowl flushing, and of hands being washed.

Dane emerged as though nothing remarkable had happened.

"Did you go to the toilet, Dane?" I asked.

"Yes, Mummy."

"And you washed your hands too?"

"Yes, Mummy."

"Oh, Dane, that's wonderful. I'm so proud of you!"

He just looked at me blankly as if he'd been using the toilet for years. He never soiled his clothes again, day or night.

Dane has a high pain threshold so when he complained of severe pain in an undescended testicle we were immediately concerned.

A specialist examined him briefly. "But why do you want your son to have treatment for this?" he asked.

I replied, "Because Dane is in pain, and they're obviously not going to descend naturally."

The specialist looked at me condescendingly. "But why create a situation where Dane could be fertile?"

"What do you mean?" I asked.

He replied irritably, "I think I've made myself quite clear."

I felt my temperature rising. "But Dane is in constant pain!"

The specialist then raised his voice and slowly enunciated each word: "Mrs. . . . Waites . . . You . . . won't . . . have . . .to . . . worry . . . if . . . your . . . son . . . will . . . be . . . fertile!"

My knees shook so violently I could hardly raise myself from the chair. On the way out I was so rattled that I actually paid the account.

Our family doctor then referred us to a kind, sensible specialist who spoke *to* Dane, not around him, in a language that he could understand. There was no question of will we or won't we operate, only how soon Dane's pain could be eliminated.

Dane was calm and cooperative at the Mercy Hospital. I was invited into the recovery room, and I stayed with him overnight. What a different experience to the one I had when I found him tied by his wrists and ankles to a hospital bed.

Dane hadn't seen snow, so we decided to celebrate his recovery with a trip to the mountains. Dane examined the snow, smelled it, tasted it, and watched the huge flakes settling on the arching branches of the trees. Then Rod suggested he might like to slide on an old raincoat we kept in the car trunk. Wow! So this is what snow is for! We had never seen Dane so eager to play as Rod dragged that raincoat up and down the hills until they were both exhausted.

That day marked so many achievements for Dane: he could use the toilet, he'd had his operation, and we were learning to channel his obsessions. Best of all, he played and laughed and tumbled with his dad like any other happy little boy. I felt so happy for Rod, who wrote: "For me, father–son interplay was something other fathers enjoyed. But not this father. That day with Dane in the snow was unique. The joy of those few hours of fun and laughter with my son warmed me for many years."

The Red Balloon was the only story Dane allowed me to read to him as a toddler. Any other book set him screaming and yet, years before his speech arrived, the story of Pascal and the balloons captivated him. He'd listen to me read *The Red Balloon* over and over again. When he developed speech I'd ask him what came next, and he'd tell me, exactly. Then he'd ask me to read the same passage, again. "You read it, Mum. You tell me."

With the exception of *The Red Balloon* Dane would only flick through a book before slamming it shut. My friends' children enjoyed Dr. Seuss so in desperation I bought *Hop on Pop* and *The Cat in the Hat* for Dane. To my delight he loved these wonderful, nonsensical rhyming stories where the three Rs meant Repetition, Rote and Rhythm!

These books were so different from *The Red Balloon* and Dane didn't like change. So what was happening? I came to believe that Dane enjoyed the Dr. Seuss books because the words sounded so different from our everyday speech. Then, as I became aware of this, I understood why he responded to my singing around the house. It was the difference in the sound of my voice that attracted his attention. So why was Dane—who intensely disliked change—responding so positively to these particular changes? I could only presume that the pleasure he derived from the repetitive rhyming helped him to overcome his fear of change.

Rod and I could not properly share Christmas with Dane until he began to communicate with us. For years, Christmas had meant nothing more to him than a pleasant meal with his cousins and grandparents. Unlike other children, he didn't experience the excitement of decorating the tree or visiting Santa at the shopping center. And to offer him a gift-wrapped package would have resulted in a screaming session.

By his seventh Christmas, though, he had begun to understand the story of Baby Jesus and the three wise men, and the bringing of gifts to the manger. We knew that, if introduced, Santa would be with us forever and we might have some explaining to do later, but we didn't want Dane's Christmases to be different from those of other children. So Rod and I decided it was time to introduce Dane to the trimmings and the excitement of Christmas.

I explained to Dane how Santa leaves gifts for children on Christmas Eve. I asked him to tell me what he would like Santa to bring him so I could write him a letter. Cautiously I added, "If he possibly can, Santa will bring it for you."

Dane's eyes opened wide. Then he took a deep breath and exclaimed, "An orange balloon!"

Grateful that Dane hadn't nominated a roomful of boxes or a large animal from the zoo, I carefully printed "orange balloon" in the letter for Santa. Then I said, "Now Dane, is there anything else you'd like? A toy truck? Some new Legos?"

He could hardly believe his good fortune. "Oh! A green balloon, too!" he gasped.

On Christmas Eve Dane hung his stocking at the foot of his bed. We explained that Santa appreciates a light supper, so after midnight Mass we placed a piece of pie and a glass of lemonade in Dane's room. After saying our prayers I told him that Santa always waits until the children fall asleep, then he brings the presents. I assumed Dane would fall asleep quickly, so not long afterward I crept into his room. I jumped with fright when out of the darkness boomed, "That you, Santa?"

I retreated hastily. This little scenario was repeated four times until "Santa" crawled in on all fours to remove the pie and lemonade.

The next morning Dane strode into our room and thundered, "What do you think? That Santa Claus! He came in when we were asleep. He stole the drink and the food and he never left anything in the stocking! No orange balloon! Nothing!"

Rod and I looked at each other dumfounded. That was the longest speech Dane had ever made. Then Rod turned to me and said severely, "Why didn't Santa bring any presents?"

I wondered aloud if perhaps he'd left the gifts in the family room. Dane made a quick exit.

Dane's fear of the unknown wouldn't allow him to open a box or unwrap a gift, but I wanted him to experience the excitement of finding a gift. So I had placed each inflated balloon in a partially opened box and balanced a piece of wrapping paper on top of each one. Dane would only have to lift the paper and raise the lids to find his gifts.

But even that proved too daunting for him. He wouldn't even touch the wrapping paper. So, very slowly, Rod lifted the paper off the first box and then raised the lid. Dane could hardly bring himself to watch.

Very gently Rod said, "See, Dane, here's your orange balloon."

As Rod withdrew the balloon from its box, Dane flinched as if in pain.

We repeated the procedure with the green balloon, and at last Dane had his first gifts from Santa. Now that they were out of their gift boxes, Dane was happy. Rod and I will always treasure the memory of that Christmas morning when we first truly shared Christmas with our son.

Later, when Dane reached his teens, we explained that Santa only leaves gifts for younger children. He was aware that Santa no longer visited his cousins and accepted this information calmly, but for a few years he'd say rather wistfully, "I'm too *old* for Santa now, aren't I, Mum?"

Any deviation from our regular daily routine was certain to upset Dane. Occasionally the change was so small that I didn't recognize it. Shortly after his eighth birthday, his table manners had improved so much that for the first time in many years I laid the table with a fresh cloth and flowers and served the milk in a jug. I then asked Dane to pass me his cup so I could pour his milk from the jug.

Dane looked at me, then at the cup, then back at me.

I repeated, "Dane. Your cup. Please pass me your cup."

He stared at me, uncomprehendingly.

I took a deep breath, and pointed to his cup. "This is your cup, Dane. Please pass it to me."

He gave me another blank stare. I couldn't understand why he wouldn't pick up his cup. The cup was familiar—he used it every day. He knew what I meant when I asked him to pick up an object and pass it to me. So why wouldn't he pass me his cup?

I knew I couldn't allow myself to become irritated with Dane; this could destroy years of work. If I calmed myself and looked for signals, this might be a defining moment.

So, what exactly was I asking him to do? Maybe I should be more specific: first ask him to pick up the cup, then secondly pass it to me.

Holding my coffee cup in the air I said, "See, Dane? This is how you pick up your cup. Now you pick up your cup."

Still he didn't respond. Very gently I pushed his cup against his clenched fingers. I did this until he took hold of it. Then he watched me intently as once again I raised and lowered my cup. He shifted his gaze to his cup, still clenched in his right hand. Slowly he raised his left hand and stroked his right hand, then the cup, and then the tablecloth. It was as if he needed to identify these three separate things: hand, cup and table. Then he looked at me as if to ask what to do next.

Placing my hand over his, I gently raised his hand, with the cup, and said, "We're picking up the cup together, Dane."

Dane gasped, and examined the bottom of the cup as though reading the manufacturer's mark. Then, as if to break some invisible thread, he tentatively passed his free hand from side to side, between the cup and the table. He seemed surprised to find an empty space.

He put his cup back on the table and stared at it for a moment or two. Then he pointed to the cup and announced, "That's the cup. The cup finishes."

The cup finishes? Whatever did this mean? Didn't he understand where the cup ended and the table began? Was he seeking reassurance that if he picked up the cup, the table wouldn't come along with it?

I struggled to answer him clearly. "Yes, Dane, the cup finishes. This is the cup and this is the table. The cup sits on the table. You can lift up the cup and pass it to me and I'll fill it with milk. Then I'll pass it back to you."

Straightaway he nodded, picked up his cup and placed it gently in my outstretched hand.

Later Rod and I puzzled over this incident. Rod asked how I usually gave Dane his milk. Rod's question helped me to understand what had happened—until that moment I had never asked Dane to pick up an empty cup. I had always poured the milk into his cup in the kitchen and then brought it to the table. On this occasion I'd changed the routine. I'd brought milk to the table in a jug, and that was the problem.

A prayer for a cowboy

I was so proud when Dane was moved into the Irabina schoolroom. This was a big change for him, and for me. He was a big boy now. The schoolroom served as a springboard for the integration of children with special needs into "special" and mainstream schools. Irabina students who were to move to new settings were integrated slowly, with short visits spaced over a number of weeks.

In the schoolroom, self-expression and social and academic skills were taught through music, reading and writing, dance and drama, story telling and songs. Humor with a strong visual impact was considered important, and Dane began to enjoy playing with water guns and balloons and "dress-ups." He began to tell the time and to read street signs, and he soon learned to identify international signs in public places. He learned to write, too, by tracing over simple sentences.

A communications book established a daily link between child, parents and teachers. This wonderfully effective device enhanced Dane's learning and clarified countless confused messages between school and home.

The teachers at Irabina understood that many children with autism have abnormal reactions to sound, touch and other stimuli. Dane was no exception. Everything he touched went straight to his mouth, then he'd sniff it. He'd shake a person's hand in greeting then sniff his own fingers. He'd giggle for no apparent reason and, if left unchecked, these episodes would gain in momentum until he lost control. Dane's teachers strongly discouraged this giggling, unless there was an obvious cause. At the first sign of a giggling episode at home, Rod and I would move him to a quiet place to help calm him. Eventually these giggling episodes diminished.

Dane still didn't appear to enjoy the company of other children. Rod and I felt that he needed a companion, so why not a dog? After much research, Rod decided on a German shorthaired pointer puppy. We gave Dane the puppy for his ninth birthday. Her name was Jaeger, meaning "huntress." We "prepared" Dane for weeks before Jaeger's arrival, showing him photographs and books, and explaining the puppy's needs.

Dane was very gentle though one day he forgot the rules and lifted Jaeger by her hind legs off the ground. Jaeger howled at the top of her lungs. Dane still screamed at the sound of a baby's cry and the puppy's howls had the same effect.

Despite this early upset, Jaeger became Dane's friend and protector. We'd wrap her leash around his wrist and together they'd ramble up and down our quiet street. One day we heard a commotion and saw Dane and Jaeger hurrying home. The dog was covered in mud, Dane less so.

Dane was distraught. He asked me why the children were being nasty. I asked him if they were being nasty to Jaeger, but he didn't think so. He thought they were being nasty to him, though he didn't know why.

Rod and I spoke to our neighbors who reported having seen youngsters throwing lumps of clay at Dane. They told us how the dog stood defiantly between the aggressive children and her young master. The children had retreated. Rod's choice of a birthday gift for his son had proved ideal.

When Margaret Whitcombe was free we'd take Dane to Mass at the Sacred Heart Monastery in Croydon where, between us, we'd generally manage to keep him occupied. Despite his challenging behavior, the priests made us feel welcome.

One Sunday I mentioned to Father Brian Gallagher how important it was to me that Dane receive Holy Communion, so Father Brian introduced us to Sister Eleanor Davis of Our Lady of the Sacred Heart Sisters. Sister Eleanor took our advice that Dane would learn more through visual clues than from the spoken word. He had a "picture-book" Bible so together they worked with this to create a special book for Dane. Sister Eleanor penciled messages into Dane's special book, and he'd write over these. By doing this he received the message and took ownership of the words.

Sister Eleanor expanded Dane's understanding of family: *Jesus has a family. The Church is Jesus' family. We become a member of this wider family when we're baptized.* She described the Last Supper with drawings and Dane began to recognize these symbols at Mass, and to discuss them afterward. He'd tell me why we say "Amen" when we receive the body of Christ, and he understood that Sister Eleanor was preparing him for this.

In his book *People Prayer, Stories of God*, Father Brian Gallagher recalls Dane's first communion (as Dane was too young to grant permission for his name to be published, Father Brian refers to him as "Damian"):

Damian is the youngest person in this book: he is only ten years old. Damian is a bright, friendly, mischievous ball of energy, constantly moving from one object of his interest to another (people, trees, animals, even insects). He loves to sing—actually more than talk! Damian is autistic.

It was hard to know how much Damian understood about God and Jesus—his parents even delayed his first receiving of Holy Communion for that reason. But, after careful preparation, finally the day for his first communion arrived.

During the celebration of Eucharist, Damian and his mother were the first to approach the priest for communion: they returned to their places in the front seats, while others, friends and relations, received communion. Without warning, the silence of the "thanksgiving time" was suddenly broken by a child's joyful singing, "Kum By Ya, My Lord, Kum By Ya."

We listened, all smiles. Damian had found his way to thank God for the gift of Jesus.

I wish I had Damian's simplicity, spontaneity, and certainty about God . . . I reckon my prayer would go ahead in leaps and bounds.

Not long after this, Margaret and I were invited to attend the ordination of a young deacon. Dane sat spellbound throughout the service and was the first to congratulate Father Paul afterward. At Mass the next day he was thrilled to see the newly ordained Father Paul who was the main celebrant. The Mass flowed beautifully and all was silent as Father Paul intoned, "Let this become the body and blood of Christ." He paused and in the silence Dane's loud voice boomed out, "I hope this works. It's his first time, you know!"

Dane had a pragmatic attitude toward God that often surprised us. One day, I waited with him at the airport to see Rod off on a business trip. As Dane happily explored the surroundings Rod and I noticed a crowd of disembarking passengers from the United States. In this crowd was a handsome, powerfully built man dressed in brightly colored western-style clothes, a huge cowboy hat and elaborate boots. He was in a wheelchair.

Dane stopped in his tracks when he saw the cowboy. He went closer to the young man and, wide-eyed, scrutinized him from head to toe. Then he carefully examined the wheelchair. The cowboy turned to Dane and gave him a friendly smile.

"You got sore leg?" Dane asked him.

The cowboy replied, "I can't use my legs anymore. I broke my back."

Dane gazed at the cowboy with a grave expression. "I'll pray for you," he said.

With tears in his eyes the cowboy replied, "And I believe you, little buddy!"

Dane's repetitive speech, or echolalia, was confusing to Rod and me, so I cannot imagine how astonishing it must have been to those new to the world of autism. I was still working at Warrawong Day Care Kindergarten as a part-time bookkeeper. When a new director, Liz Gower, started at the kindergarten, I introduced her to Dane. Meeting Dane was Liz Gower's first contact with autism. They had a brief conversation and then, while he settled on a chair outside her office to wait for me, she went back to work. Minutes later she heard the sound of voices outside her office. She was astonished to hear Dane repeating their entire conversation. He was word perfect, and he reproduced exactly her intonations, expressions, reactions—everything!

Liz realized that Dane's repetition was simply his way of organizing his thought processes, of trying to assimilate her into his scheme of things. She recognized that for Dane everything must be orderly: *This is how Mrs. Gower speaks. This is what Mrs. Gower said.*

Liz Gower's perceptive observations helped Rod and me come to terms with Dane's echolalia. We knew his ability to repeat entire conversations demonstrated an extraordinary memory and mimicking skills. On the other hand, we were acutely aware that to simply marvel at these skills would have been futile. So could we use these memory and mimicking skills to help Dane?

Liz explained how echolalia offered us a communication tool to work with. She could see that at times Dane used his echolalia in an attempt to communicate with us. We learned to listen to these repetitions and expand on what we'd hear. For example, Dane would ask, "What color are the clouds?" and he'd insist that we reply, "White, with a silver lining." So we began to alter our replies. If the day was overcast, we'd say, "The clouds are gray today, Dane; it might rain." For weeks he'd scream when we changed the echolalic response that he was expecting. Eventually, however, he began to understand and accept that by changing our response we were giving him information.

Dane continued to mimic other children's mannerisms and voices. He did this in his thinking aloud and in his day-to-day activity. In order to overcome it, we'd ask, "Who are you, Dane?" Initially, he'd be reluctant to respond but we'd persist until he answered with his own name, using his own voice. Then we'd exclaim, "What lovely talking. We like listening to Dane!"

We had to make him understand that we wouldn't accept other children's voices or mannerisms. "Dane, you're not Peter," we'd admonish him. Or, "Dane, you're not Troy." After months of these reminders he began to observe, "I'm not Peter, am I?" "I'm not Troy." He had great difficulty separating his responses and attitudes from those of his peers.

For years, Dane couldn't eat a meal in public. I couldn't even stop in a shopping center for a cool drink; this would reduce him to a screaming heap.

This behavior had to stop. I began pausing at quick service counters, explaining to Dane that I was going to drink some orange juice and that I wouldn't be long. (I couldn't offer him any juice because that would provoke more screams.)

I'd talk him through each stage: "Dane, I'm buying an orange juice. I'm drinking my orange juice. I'm enjoying my orange juice." Nervous bystanders would move aside.

Dane began to accept that drinking the juice didn't take too long. On each occasion I'd take a little more time and drink a little more juice. After many months of this routine, I could drink all my juice. He still wouldn't accept a drink for himself, becoming very upset if I tried to insist.

My next step was to venture into a coffee shop. I'd select a table near the exit so Dane didn't feel confined, and I'd seat him against a wall so he couldn't bump other customers. I'd order an orange drink, we'd sit at the table for a few moments, then we'd move on. Again, I gradually began to linger over my drink. When he became accustomed to this, I started ordering small, fast-food snacks that he might share.

Dane's first mouthful of food in a coffee shop was a real achievement! He finally accepted the notion of eating and drinking in unfamiliar surroundings. Eventually I was "allowed" to order a drink for him, a coffee for myself and a snack for us to share. What a relief that was.

Very slowly we moved Dane on from coffee shops to a restaurant. When Dane appeared ready for this change, Rod and I went to see the manager of Il Gambero, a restaurant where Rod often ate when he was working late. We told him about Dane and his needs. The restaurant had solid refectory tables and long wooden pews. We asked if Dane could stand on a seat near the window and watch the traffic.

The manager agreed and assured us we'd be welcomed warmly, and thus began our friendship with Il Gambero, a friendship that's still in place today. The staff made us feel like honored guests. They made a fuss over Dane but they soon learned to recognize his many moods and knew when to stand back.

Initially Rod and I would order simple, quick-serve meals. We ate while Dane looked out the window, then we'd leave. After some weeks Dane would accept a mouthful of our pasta, and eventually we could eat our meal a little more slowly and feed him from our plates. One momentous evening we ordered a serving just for Dane. At last he felt comfortable and understood exactly why we were here. We were here to eat pasta! So he ate his pasta too.

After twelve months of regular visits to Il Gambero we introduced Dane to another restaurant. Again we explained our mission to the manager, and again we were promised a warm welcome. At home we pretended we were visiting this new restaurant. We showed him how we'd sit on individual chairs, not wooden pews. We explained how the menu would be written on thick paper and not a blackboard, and how it would take us longer to read this new menu. We acted out the waiter's questions and our replies. We demonstrated with a clock that the meals would take longer to cook and to serve.

Dane soon learned to accept this restaurant too. Then week by week we'd alternate Il Gambero with other restaurants. While Il Gambero remained our favorite, the succession of different restaurants helped Dane accept change and relate to other people. It helped to break through his autistic insistence that everything remain exactly the same. It was as if he was learning to build on each new experience. Eating out with Dane was very important to Rod and me too. It offered us an opportunity to relax as a couple, and as a family, and this helped us to cope.

One day, at the end of his long introduction to restaurants, Dane and I joined Rod for lunch at the Windsor Hotel. Rod often entertained clients at this elegant Melbourne landmark and the staff knew him well. The waiters paid special attention to Dane, who appeared to enjoy the pomp and ceremony. Suddenly, in the middle of lunch and using his biggest voice, Dane announced proudly, "There's no other children here, Mum!"

An apple for the man

Rod and I were aware that Irabina's primary function was to help younger children with autism develop their potential so they could move into the wider community, mostly through "special" schools. So when Dane was around ten and a half, we weren't surprised when his teacher told us that the time had come for him to leave Irabina. He was to move on to a larger school where he would receive further stimulation to increase his skills.

It wasn't easy to find a school with teachers qualified to instruct children with autism. The Bulleen Special School, a state school for students with disabilities, seemed to suit Dane's needs best, and the staff there were prepared to implement a transition program with Irabina for Dane. They were very accepting of and interested in Irabina's programs. There was no hint of "we'll do it our way, thank you!"

Bulleen had a one-to-ten student-teacher ratio, but I soon realized that Dane, and other young students with autism, needed an extra teacher. With other parents, I approached our Education Minister to ask for help. An extra teacher was allocated, and this enabled Bulleen Special School to develop valuable expertise in the field of autism.

Dane's enrollment procedure at Bulleen included routine testing. After the tests, the doctor asked me, rather severely, why I'd ignored my son's very poor vision. I protested, telling him about Dane's annual eye tests by a specialist in whom we had the utmost confidence. The school doctor recommended a second opinion.

This didn't make sense. Doctors had ordered eye tests when Dane was nine months old to ascertain if the deep forceps mark that closed his left eye after his birth had affected his eyesight. The tests revealed his sight was normal but to allay our on-going concern we took him for annual checks.

Dane detested the eye drops he'd be given at these annual checks. We hadn't learned the art of "preparing" him back then. We hadn't learned to say, "Dane, the doctor will put drops in your eyes. They might feel cold and your eyes will feel different for a while." We hadn't learned to "practice" putting in eye drops with over-the-counter drops. So each year I'd drag him back and try to communicate with the specialist above the screams.

We wasted no time getting the second opinion. Extensive tests showed that Dane had severe myopia and acute astigmatism. We were told that an operation when he was eight could have helped to correct his problems but that it was too late now.

Missing this opportunity to improve Dane's eyesight preyed on my mind. Granted our visits to the previous specialist were noisy and disruptive but why hadn't he suggested this operation? Had I misheard him? I felt so guilty and upset that I arranged for another consultation with the original specialist. No, there was no misunderstanding or misdiagnosis. This man had simply chosen not to mention the operation because he thought we had enough problems already. Once again a specialist had chosen to play God and as a result Dane faced life-long visual impairment.

Around this time, Rod's need for my support expanded along with his ever-increasing business commitments. So we began to look for readily available overnight respite care for Dane. We couldn't constantly impose our growing need for care on our dear friends. They were already giving us so much wonderful support.

Respite care "on demand" is a priority for all parents of children with special needs, but in our case this didn't come easily. First we tried Interchange Victoria (Respite Care), a scheme that seeks to match children with disabilities with a host family. Despite our best efforts, Dane's autism meant we could not find a suitable family.

We then investigated a government funded Community Respite Unit (CRU) where groups of children are cared for. We thought it might be good for Dane to interact with other youngsters away from school and home.

After Dane's first overnight stay at the unit, we noticed a nasty cut on his hand. A supervisor explained how, unnoticed by the staff, he had found some bottles and smashed them. Rod and I discovered a pile of broken glass outside the building. We were shocked and surprised that Dane had been unsupervised long enough for him to slip away and break the bottles, and that the broken glass had not been cleaned up.

After this stay, Dane regressed badly in his behavior and speech. We spent almost two weeks easing him back into a comfortable daily routine. However, we decided to give the CRU a second chance, choosing a weekend when another boy from Dane's school would be staying there too. We hoped this might help but we were so wrong.

Dane was vague and irrational on our drive home from this second stay. I encouraged him to talk about his weekend but he couldn't find the words, nor did we have any point of reference to communicate with him. Then I remembered that the supervisor had mentioned they might visit a park. So I said, "I hope you visited the park, Dane. That must have been fun!"

Straightaway we had his attention. "Yes," he said, "and I had a drink of beer!"

"You had a drink of what, Dane?"

"Beer."

"That was ginger beer, was it, Dane?"

"No, Mum. I had Fosters out of a can!"

Rod asked, "Where did you find the Fosters can, Dane?"

"The bus driver gave it to me. He gave me some of his Fosters."

We were too upset to investigate this incident any further. Needless to say Dane never stayed there again.

Months later we discovered the Southern Autistic Centre at Mentone. To our relief, this excellent center offered respite care for children with autism. The well-trained staff were attuned to the needs of children like Dane and his experience here was very different. We'll never know if Dane actually enjoyed those stays at Mentone but his behavior didn't regress. To us, this indicated that all was well.

Shortly after Dane's eleventh birthday we decided to move from our spacious home in leafy Croydon to a townhouse in Brunswick, an inner-Melbourne suburb. After years of long, tiring drives between Croydon and the city, we now lived about ten minutes by car from Rod's office, and were much closer to Dane's new school.

This was a momentous change for Dane to face, and he appeared to handle it more easily than we'd expected. The century-old Brunswick house emanated warmth and charm. Dane was attracted to the stained-glass windows, one of which featured a golden sun, steep sided mountains, and a tree! Lavish plasterwork adorned the ceilings and on the one in Dane's bedroom we picked out the fruit and flowers in the pattern in different colors. This became an instant source of entertainment for him.

In Brunswick, we discovered that the local council's home care service employed two women with special-needs training, both of whom looked after Dane from time to time, thus freeing me to do things like helping Rod entertain business associates. Each of these remarkable women achieved wonderful results with Dane. They expanded his areas of interest, they made him laugh, and they always left him in a happy frame of mind.

But it was our neighbors who made Brunswick so very special for us. Mostly Italian, these warm and vibrant people welcomed us with open arms into their community. Here, in this village within a city, we felt no need to apologize for our son's behavior.

To our new neighbors, Dane was "Dano." They loved his broad smile and accepted his eccentricities without question. Caterina Gentile from over the road would exclaim, "So none of us are perfect! We've all got a problem!"

Sammy and Santina lived in the adjoining house. Sammy spoke little English; he and Dane communicated best with their eyes and hands. Dane loved to watch Sammy making the sausage and pasta and tasty sauces that they insisted on sharing with us. One day, when I was describing where we lived to Dane's teacher, she laughed and said, "I thought you might live next to a food-processing factory! Dane is always talking about the delicious pasta and sauces and sausage he's helped to make."

With Dane, Rod and I made the most of everything this cosmopolitan neighborhood had to offer. We all enjoyed the Italian music and culture and, especially, the food. On Friday evenings we'd take turns choosing which enticing restaurant we'd sample next. On warm summer evenings we'd often buy takeout treats from Lygon Street's delicatessens, and enjoy the cool and quiet of Melbourne's beautiful parks. We'd find a quiet spot so Dane could think aloud without intruding on other people's privacy.

Despite his new friendships, Dane's intense dislike of crowds persisted. If someone bumped him in the street, he'd glare at them angrily. So Rod and I wondered how he would cope with the Lygon Street Festival, Melbourne's annual celebration of Italian culture. With Lygon Street only a short distance from our home, we'd be almost in the thick of the happy, boisterous activities.

We prepared Dane as best we could, trying to describe the crowds and the noise and the activity, and explaining that all this would be part of having fun. And Dane did enjoy the festival. He reveled in the color, the excitement, the music and, in particular, the endless choice of Italian food! He accepted an occasional bump from another person as part of the fun. He understood this was an occasion to share with our Italian neighbors. Time and again he exclaimed, "This is our festival! This is where we live!"

Dane also didn't seem to mind the cheering, yelling crowds at our local soccer field, as he would eagerly accompany Rod to the matches. Rod would make sure they arrived only for the last quarter of the match; this was all Dane could cope with. They'd take a ball along, and after the game finished they'd jump the fence onto the field and join the crowd of spectators playing "kick to kick."

When Rod recorded his thoughts about these soccer matches, he wrote: "I'd kick the ball to Dane and he'd mark it, and then he'd kick the guts out of it! Then I'd fox the ball through the crowd and look around, and he'd be frozen to the spot where I'd left him. He couldn't relax and be part of this human tide of enjoyment. We'd do this for half an hour or so and then we'd walk home. It amazed me that every week he really looked forward to this!"

Sometimes I'd watch Rod and Dane kicking their ball on the field. I'd see a thousand and one people in that crowd. The thousand would all be interacting with one another—shouting encouragement, teasing and bantering, and just letting off steam. It was so dismally easy for me to identify the "one."

A chance encounter with a homeless man on one of our summer evening outings showed us that Dane was becoming more aware of the people around him. We were in Melbourne's Exhibition Gardens having a picnic when we noticed Dane gazing intently at a shabbily dressed man sitting quietly on a bench nearby.

"Why is that man with the bags wearing all those clothes? Why is he having dinner by himself?" he asked.

Rod and I answered that the man probably had no home or parents. We explained why he had to wear all his clothes or carry them in the plastic bags. Dane listened quietly but we were unsure how much he understood.

We continued eating and Dane carefully selected an apple from the picnic basket. Placing the apple to one side he insisted we not eat it. Very gently, I tried to reassure him that there was nothing wrong with the apple.

Emphatically Dane replied, "No, Mum, I'm going to give the apple to the man."

We were delighted, though Rod warned Dane to be cautious. "Don't embarrass the man, Dane. Just hold up the apple and let him see that we're leaving it for him. Let him choose whether or not he wants the apple."

As we left the park Dane placed the apple on the bench we'd been sitting on and, looking toward the man and pointed to the apple. The man gave Dane a slight acknowledgment, which satisfied him.

From then on Dane always reminded me to bring something for the people who lived in the park.

Around this time I began to feel the need to do something for myself. Since Dane's birth I had devoted my entire life to his welfare. Apart from taking care of his physical needs, almost every waking moment had been spent creating appropriate and acceptable situations for him, checking out options, and struggling to retain existing services or working toward having new ones set up. I was in danger of losing my own identity and needed to do something about it. But what?

The answer lay right outside our front door. Our wonderful Italian neighbors were doing their utmost to communicate with us in English. Why not meet them halfway?

I enrolled in Italian classes at the university. Our neighbors were delighted with my humble efforts. I felt honored when Caterina offered to lend me her son's very first books. She had carried these books in her luggage from Italy. Before long the neighborhood was using fractured Italian, throwing in some English to help things along! We didn't strive for perfection, but we had a lot of fun.

At age eleven Dane still showed very little affection. The exception to this was Jaeger. Jaeger was always Dane's dog. He fed her, and helped me to bath her and clean her kennel. He was always quick to ask, "Can Jaeger come?" She imposed no pressure on him. She never asked for more than he was prepared to offer. She just loved him, and he'd stroke her head and allow her to place her head in his lap.

In turn, Jaeger was possessive of us all. One evening we were driving with Dane and Jaeger in the back seat when a police car flashed its blue lights. Rod pulled over and lowered the window as an officer approached. Bristling with irritation, the officer slapped his hand on the car door and glared through the window at Rod. Immediately Jaeger lunged over Rod's right shoulder, all growls and teeth! The officer leapt backward and visibly paled as Jaeger snarled through the open window. Somewhat shakily, he signalled Rod to drive on.

Jaeger wasn't a noisy dog so when she broke into a frenzy one afternoon, I rushed outdoors to investigate. She was barking furiously at a man on our roof; he was carrying a bag, which we later found out was filled with valuables from a nearby house.

I ran to fetch Sammy. In his seventies and about five foot nothing, dear Sammy stood on the footpath and harangued the trespasser in his most colorful Italian. With Sammy at the front and Jaeger going crazy at the back, the thief wasn't going anywhere so I phoned the police. I think he was quite relieved to be escorted away in one piece.

Jaeger wasn't vicious, but I'm certain she would have retaliated had anyone tried to approach Dane. When we were confident Dane knew his way around the new neighborhood, we would let him take Jaeger for walks. With Jaeger by his side, Dane's different behaviors and thinking aloud became less obvious. He became just another young man walking his dog.

Dane continued to have obsessions, but Rod and I were learning to work with them, not against them. Before we left Croydon, Dane had developed a preference for turning left whenever we drove along a major road. He'd become increasingly agitated each time we turned right. Rod wondered if this was related to his walking counterclockwise around the table as a toddler.

By the time we moved to Brunswick, Dane's preference for turning left had became a full-blown obsession. If we dared to turn right off a major road or a freeway, he'd break into screams of frustration. We tried to divert his attention away from left and right by encouraging him to read the road signs. This made matters worse until one day it dawned on us that every few miles there were signs saying "Trucks Left

Lane" or "Trucks Merge Left for Detour." We realized that Dane wanted us to follow the trucks.

So Rod formulated a plan to work with the obsession. He took Dane to visit trucking depots where he pointed out the individual makes of trucks: Kenworth, Mack, Mercedes, Volvo and so on. They walked around the trucks, listened to the noises they made and peered into the cabins. Rod hoped that by learning to identify the trucks, Dane's obsession with left turns would diminish and, thankfully, he was correct. Soon Dane was exclaiming, "That's a Mack!" or "That's a Kenworth!" and this gave him a very real sense of achievement.

For Rod and me, spot the truck was far more acceptable than turn left or else!

One Sunday we all drove to an isolated beach at Dromana on Melbourne's Mornington Peninsula. Rod and I spread a rug on grassy parkland beside the beach. While we relaxed in the afternoon sunshine, we watched Dane running about with Jaeger on a leash as she bounded from place to place. The shadows lengthened and we decided to have some coffee before driving home. We had hardly taken our eyes off Dane and Jaeger all afternoon, but when I looked up from pouring the coffee, they had gone. Open grassland and beach surrounded us, but there was no sign of Dane or his dog.

Frantically we searched for him. I felt nauseous with apprehension. I could see light traffic moving along the highway, but that was some distance from where we'd been having our picnic. Surely Dane couldn't have moved that far so quickly? We ran to the highway but he wasn't there.

Rod suggested I go back and wait at the picnic area in case Dane went back there. Rod was right, of course, but I felt so useless. I desperately needed to do something—anything!

Meanwhile Rod ran across the highway into a small shop. He explained to the shopkeeper that our son was missing.

"How long has your son been gone?" the shopkeeper asked kindly.

"About ten minutes," Rod replied.

The shopkeeper's expression changed from sympathy to incredulity. "And you want to phone the police already?"

Hastily Rod described Dane's condition and, somewhat grudgingly, the shopkeeper indicated his telephone.

Rod called the police. Their response horrified him. The officer he spoke to was adamant that no assistance could be given until Dane had been missing for at least one hour. That was the rule. Ignoring Rod's frantic pleas the officer suggested we keep looking and phone again in an hour if we were still worried.

An hour? One hour's delay could mean life or death to a young boy, while police talk about rules!

It was almost nightfall, and I felt numb with misery and cold when Rod came back. Earlier we had noticed another couple walking on the beach. They were just specks in the distance now, but Rod ran off after them. He then ran all the way back with the news that they hadn't seen Dane either.

Helplessly I waited in the picnic area while Rod rushed about in all directions, shouting for Dane. He was drenched in sweat and we were both shaking with fright. He kept looking at his watch and the very moment one hour expired, he burst into that store like a bank robber.

Rod made his second call to the police and within minutes a patrol car appeared, sirens wailing and lights flashing. As the police began to question us, a car traveling on the other side of the road made a U-turn and pulled up.

"Excuse me," said the driver, "are you looking for a blond-haired boy with a dog?"

My stomach lurched.

Rod replied, "Yes, we are!"

"Well he's down the road heading for the city. I offered him a lift but the dog wouldn't let me near!"

Rod leapt into our car and followed that kind man back along the highway until he found Dane and Jaeger calmly walking along the road in the dark. I stayed with the police until we all knew that Dane was safe.

Later, when we were discussing the incident with Dane, he told us that he had heard our frantic calls.

"Why didn't you answer us?" we asked.

He replied, "But I knew where you were."

It was enough for Dane that he could hear us calling him. He had no concept that he should respond. He was completely oblivious to our anguish. We asked Dane if he'd got lost on the beach, but he told us no, he'd walked to the road to count the cars going past. Then he'd decided to walk toward the city lights. He knew we lived near those lights and, given his excellent navigation skills, I dare say he would have found his way home.

For years shopping with Dane had been almost impossible. We couldn't pass a cardboard carton or pause beside a supermarket shelf without a screaming session ensuing. However, as Dane's social skills improved, we gradually introduced him to supermarkets.

At first we'd make just one purchase. I'd tell him what we were going to buy and why we needed it. We'd select the item quickly and hurry through an express lane. I'd hand over the correct change without waiting for a receipt. Then we'd buy two items, then three. I'd always include something we could share and enjoy when we got home. Dane loved dried apples, smoked oysters, pâté and dips. I would buy something different each time so as not to create another obsession.

At this stage, I dared not forget anything. Despite his age and size, Dane would stand in the cart, his feet at the back, his hands leaning on the front bar, and insist that we go forward. I couldn't pull that cart backward, no matter how slightly. We'd take exactly the same route up and down the aisles every time, and I'd have to be quick—to let Dane climb out of the cart was to invite disaster.

After months of this I encouraged him to climb out of the cart when we'd finished our shopping and push it to the checkout stand. Then I'd ask him to climb back into the cart and hand each item to me. I had to keep him busy each and every second. I couldn't allow my attention to wander for an instant.

As Dane became more comfortable with supermarkets I was anxious for him to make a purchase alone. One day I suggested he buy a carton of milk at our corner store. I knew I could watch him unobserved as he walked to and from this store. I'd spoken to the owners about my plans to send Dane shopping alone, and they were pleased to help.

I chose a day when Dane was very calm and cooperative and said to him, "Oh, Dane, we need more milk. Will you go to the shop and buy a carton of milk for me, please?"

Dane's face brightened as he agreed to do this. I gave him the correct money and repeated what it was that I wanted. I could see he felt proud to be running an errand on his own.

After that initial success, I began to ask Dane to go to the store for three or four small items. Then I introduced the concept of accepting change. I'd give him a little extra money and remind him to wait for the change.

As Dane approached his teens, I recognized that shopping alone was a valuable tool for relieving his growing anxiety and depression. His self-esteem had diminished with the onset of puberty. A pattern emerged where his negative and uncooperative moods led to extremely difficult outbursts. I learned that if I could divert this negativity, we could usually avoid the outbursts. When I sensed a drop in his morale, I would suggest something positive for him to do. It only needed to be something simple—like walking Jaeger or going shopping.

I'd tell Dane that I would be so grateful and pleased if he would go to the store for me. Straightaway he'd brighten up and off he'd go. I always hoped he'd meet a neighbor on his way home. Often they'd invite him into their homes to share a cold drink or a hot chocolate, and they never failed to let me know where he was. Their affection and good humor was constant. Even on bad days, Dane nearly always arrived home with a smile.

Dane was having money-handling lessons at school, and these shopping expeditions helped reinforce what he was learning there. We also tried to help him recognize different coins. This involved a lot of work with big, clearly illustrated books. And when I took him shopping with me, I'd show him how much money I was handing over, and how much the cashier gave me in change. Dane began to understand that a carton of milk, for example, cost a small amount of money while a car cost a very large amount.

Dane was making progress, taking slow and steady steps into the busy life surrounding him, but his diminishing self-esteem concerned me greatly.

Master of the circles

While it seemed that Dane had coped with our move from Croydon to Brunswick, his transition from Irabina to Bulleen Special School had been a different matter. Dane experienced long-term difficulties adjusting to this change. He had been a "big boy" at Irabina and had felt comfortable in the small, protected environment. Bulleen was much larger, with an atmosphere closer to that of a conventional state school, and for Dane was not a happy place to be. "Why do I have to go there?" he'd plead with us. "What am I doing?"

Dane's dreadful tantrums continued into puberty, and the worst ones usually occurred on the way to school, and always on the same stretch of freeway. He never lost control on any other section of road, nor on our drive back home. I could not establish a pattern for these tantrums. He'd scream every day for a week, maybe longer, then he'd stop for one day, or two days, or perhaps for a month. On the good days we'd travel to Bulleen without a care in the world.

The bad days were terrifying. Dane screamed and thrashed about in the back seat of the car as though possessed. I couldn't control him. At twelve he was taller and stronger than I was. By the time we arrived at school, I'd have a pounding headache and Dane would be so distraught that I couldn't get him out of the car. I'd comb my hair, take a deep breath and, leaving Dane in the car, walk to the principal's office.

The principal always greeted me courteously, ignoring my shaking knees and hands as I asked him to help me get Dane out of the car. He would chat pleasantly as we walked to the car, then he'd open the door and speak quietly to Dane. "Come on now, Dane, it's time for school."

Every time Dane would say, "Yes, Mr. Hogg," and step out of the car as if he were the best-behaved boy in school. Then they'd walk side by side toward the school, chatting like old friends, and I'd feel like such a dope.

Erin Young had followed Dane from Irabina to Bulleen, and their weekend activities together provided him with a welcome diversion from his problems. Together they attended 808 Doncaster, a government-funded youth club for young people with special needs. With the youth club they enjoyed many activities like tenpin bowling, bush walking and horseback riding. The leaders were young and energetic, and Erin and Dane always enjoyed being a part of this team.

However, Dane's behavior continued to deteriorate. Time after time he would become belligerent and uncooperative and then fall into a dreadful depression. Nobody could reach him. Rod and I decided to seek professional help.

We attended an autism-related address given by a psychiatrist called Dr. John. Dr. John's message was clear: professionals in the field of autism should always work with the child's parents. "Remember," he urged, "the parents are your best co-therapists."

We believed Dr. John could help us, so we made an appointment to see him. He spoke with us at length, as a family, and followed this up with a series of consultations alone with Dane. He established that Dane was having difficulties with the three huge changes in his life: his move from Irabina to Bulleen, the onset of puberty, and the dramatic change in his daily routine caused by our move from Croydon to Brunswick. He suggested a course of medication for Dane.

I was reluctant to agree at first. In an effort to calm him, Dane had been medicated as a child at the Royal Children's Hospital. The medication had had the opposite effect and he had literally climbed the hospital walls. But Dr. John assured me this wouldn't happen again, and so we agreed to try it.

Dr. John suggested that we didn't mention Dane's new medication program to his teachers. He wanted any observations of changes in Dane's behavior to be totally objective.

Within three days Dane's behavior altered. His teachers approached me, saying how much calmer he was. They described how he was sitting on his chair and concentrating, and attending to tasks. They didn't ask if he was medicated. If they guessed, they didn't say so.

Since he was a toddler, Dane had enjoyed "being the wind," and there were times when we would allow him to keep on flapping his leaves or pieces of paper—times when I urgently needed some peace, or when I sensed Dane needed to be calm. However, I decided to ask Dr. John if we should try to eliminate this obsession.

His reply was that it might not be a good idea to try to eliminate Dane's obsessions; reduce them, yes, and have a cue in place to control them, but be aware that if we managed to eliminate an obsession, Dane would need something else in its place to help him feel calm. We could end up with something far more inconvenient.

Dane's echolalia became more pronounced as he approached his teens. Rod recalls a startling incident that occurred when he arrived home from work one evening:

> *As I walked past Dane's room I overheard two young lads having a very involved conversation. Not wanting to intrude, I walked through to the kitchen and said hello to Junee and asked, "Who's with Dane?"*
> *"Nobody," she replied. "Dane's on his own."*
> *"No," I said, "there's at least two others in there. I heard their conversation!"*
>
> *Junee insisted he was alone but I wouldn't be convinced: the inflections of each voice were so different and the overlapping conversation flowed so quickly.*
>
> *We walked down the hallway and as we knocked on Dane's door, Junee looked at me apologetically—now she could hear the different voices too.*
>
> *Dane called "Come in" and we opened the door. He was sitting on his bed—alone. It was scary. Absolutely scary!*

Rod had heard Dane repeating conversations before—this wasn't new—Dane had begun repeating conversations from Irabina shortly after his speech arrived. But now his echolalia had become so acute that not only did he repeat the conversation, he also copied—exactly—each speaker's tones and inflections. As Rod described, Dane carried out these impersonations with one "speaker" interrupting and over-riding the other exactly as occurs in actual conversation.

By the onset of puberty, Dane's "thinking aloud" became an essential part of his daily routine. He'd always enjoyed a quiet time in the late afternoon. Now he would use this time to review the day's conversations and events. By thinking aloud, he'd consider and review any changes to his routine, and any decisions he'd made. In time, we grew to understand that thinking aloud is Dane's way of sorting the day's information into an orderly bundle, and filing it all away for future reference.

While Dr. John's medication worked wonders for Dane's behavior, we were still concerned about his self-esteem. We looked around for ways to boost it, and wondered if learning to ride his bike in the traffic would help.

Dane had no road sense, and we knew we would have to teach him the road rules, and how to deal with dense city traffic. Finding a quiet space to practice, however, wasn't easy. Then Rod remembered the uncovered storm channel running beside the freeway.

Rod and I would prepare Dane for each ride. *This is what we'll do, Dane. This is where we'll go.* Then, having checked that no rain was forecast, we'd lower our bikes into the channel and ride for hours along its endless smooth surface. Rod led, Dane followed and I'd bring up the rear.

We'd fly along at great speed and then we'd slow to a crawl. We'd practice riding in a perfectly straight line—Dane loved this exercise! Then Rod began to indicate left and right turns and stop signals, and we'd copy his actions. Dane was determined to ride on the roads so he really wanted to learn these rules.

After months in the storm channel we became sufficiently confident to venture onto quiet roads. As Dane became more confident we moved into busier traffic. Eventually, bicycle riding became a wonderful family outing.

For a Sunday treat, we'd ride to a park. We'd picnic beside the lake there and watch people flying kites. Dane would walk around and around the water's edge, enjoying the kites and the trees. Rod would relax while I read poetry aloud. These idyllic times were a wonderful respite from our hectic weekdays. Another favorite outing was to ride along the shoreline and watch the big ships and the fishermen.

As Dane became more experienced, we encouraged him to ride around our block while we waited on the pavement. Then we'd allow him to ride alone to nearby Princes Park and back again. This gave him a wonderful sense of freedom and raised his level of confidence.

About a month before his thirteenth birthday, Dane was admitted to a hospital for allergy testing. He suffered from a mild form of asthma and for some time he'd been displaying some very odd behavior. Like a happy drunk, he'd lurch and stumble, his speech would become slurred, and he'd break into fits of giggling. Then he'd struggle to breathe.

These episodes usually took place in the car and, although mild in comparison to his screaming, they were very unnerving. Through trial and error I discovered certain foods appeared to trigger the attacks, so our local doctor sent him to be tested for allergic reactions.

The allergy unit's doors were firmly closed to the outside world. Perfume, aftershave, tobacco, shampoo, newspapers, smelly clothes—anything likely to cause a reaction was banned from this sterile, dust-free area. The water was distilled and the air was filtered six times an hour.

I knew that Dane would have to undergo a detoxifying fast, but I had assumed this would be for twenty-four hours not four long days and nights! I couldn't have begun to imagine the physical and emotional trauma of that seemingly endless nightmare. Dane screamed at me for food and begged to be taken home. He couldn't understand why we were forcing him to endure this misery.

On the morning of the fifth day Dane was allowed to eat pears. Just pears. He didn't react to these, so pears were checked as safe. The next day he was allowed sea perch. Sea perch for breakfast, morning tea, lunch, afternoon tea and dinner! Each day a different food was tried, with each reaction being carefully noted.

Simple written records helped Dane adjust to different routines, so I helped him compile a diary while he was in the allergy unit:

I was happy to see Erin my friend. I had celery. Tested apples today. The shower is broken. I had grapes for breakfast. I made a vase in crafts. Dad told me Mummy is painting the floor. I tested yellow dye. I had rabbit. I can drink tap water. I tested millet. I had a pillow fight with Dad. I tested milk. The caterpillar ate my carrots at home. I tested plastic. I tested foam. I tested rubber. The chemicals made me very silly. I did lots of work with Mummy. Dad gave me five balloons. I tested newspaper. I had a bad reaction. I tested formaldehyde and chlorine. I watched the vet on TV in a show that had a scorpion. I tested polyester and mineral thinners. Margaret and Uncle Bill and Dad came to visit. Dad went to sleep on my bed. I tested rice. I tested diesel. I tested gas and turpentine. I made my own bed. I tested candida drops. Erin gave me tapes. Ga rang up. Liz came and we had lots of fun. I tested tap water. I need to filter my water. I had hamburgers for lunch. I tested perfume. It made me very silly. I tested carpet. I tested milk and wheat. I rang Mummy and Dad and gave them a nice surprise.

His entries are interspersed with cards and letters from many thoughtful friends. Erin wrote to him about school:

Yesterday we bought axolotls. They are a walking fish. We named them Fred and Wilma. We went to Sally's

grade to see her new fish. Their names are Kev, Trev and
Lyn. See you soon.
Love Erin
P.S. How did you fit in six bananas for breakfast?

As our local doctor had suspected, Dane's immune system was damaged. We learned this may have occurred during the first few months of his life, certainly during his first two years when he had repeated courses of antibiotics for ear, nose and throat infections.

It was discovered that Dane was allergic to petrochemicals and to tartrazine, a yellow food coloring commonly used in fishsticks and snack food. Each time these products were introduced, he would almost climb the glass walls of the purpose-built testing chamber.

Dane's reaction to petrochemicals puzzled me. I couldn't understand why he didn't react badly every time we drove on the freeways. The staff explained how a multitude of other chemicals would build up in his body until his immune system was strained to the limit. With added exposure to tartrazine or petrochemicals, his system would collapse—hence the odd behavior and asthma attacks.

We asked the allergy unit staff if we should move from our inner city home to the country, or the seaside, but they said no. Rather, we should discard all household and garden chemicals and any foods with artificial flavorings, colorings or preservatives—everything that might place Dane's immune system under pressure. If we allowed his immune system to repair by reducing his exposure to these unnecessary chemicals, then he'd cope with petrochemicals on the freeways. Thankfully most food manufacturers had already bowed to public pressure for content labeling. I'll be forever grateful to those individuals who bravely confronted big business and governments on this issue.

I was also told that for several months I should rotate all the food in Dane's diet. If we had pears one day, for example, we should avoid pears for the next four or five days. My shopping list became a highly complicated forward planner!

The combination of this rotation diet and a dramatic reduction in his exposure to chemicals strengthened Dane's immune system and diminished his allergic reactions. He quickly learned to recognize the dangers of snack foods and soft drinks. "I don't really need this, do I, Mum?" he'd exclaim. "There are lots of other things I can have!"

Thus began a lifetime of seeking out chemical-free foods and drinks. He still queries every new food product I bring home. "Is this natural, Mum?"

Despite the Allergy Unit's successful outcome, we continued to live in the shadow of constantly recurring crises. There were many days when Dane would become so distraught and his behavior so disruptive that we'd be asked to withdraw him from school—sometimes for days—until he regained his composure. Dr. John had moved, so we couldn't ask him to reassess Dane's medication.

One such crisis occurred during a long dry summer. Every afternoon I would collect Dane from exactly the same place. It was outdoors and I completely forgot to say, "Now don't forget, Dane. Go into the waiting room if it rains."

Inevitably, heavy rain did fall one afternoon and a teacher moved Dane into the waiting room. Dane objected strenuously. Not only was he being removed from the place where Mum had said to stand, this waiting room also served as a time-out space for students needing to calm down. Not surprisingly, Dane interpreted the teacher's instruction to move as a punishment, and he erupted.

Time and time again misunderstandings like this came out of nowhere, and the situation would blow apart. When, occasionally, I'd meet friends and they'd talk about their teenagers' soccer and ballet and computer games, I'd be silently praying that Dane would survive the day at school.

Rod and I began to disconnect from the real world, to feel alone. We were happily married with supportive friends and family, so how could we be lonely? Only the parents of another child with autism could really understand, and only then could I open up and share the pain. Such opportunities were few and far between, but this was about to change. A very special person was about to enter our lives.

I was delighted when Bulleen Special School held an autism-specific information day for staff and parents. We were all so hungry for autism-related information. The key-note speaker was Vicki Bitsika, a psychologist employed by Alpha Terrace, a branch of the Autistic Citizens Residential and Resources Society of Victoria.

Vicki Bitsika was young and vital with a smile that lit up the room. Her advice was profoundly sensible and I wondered if I could meet her personally. A few days later, to my delight, she called out to me in the school parking lot. She was visiting in her professional capacity and had heard that Dane was having problems.

Vicki explained how she helped young people prepare for work and develop life and social skills. Dane quickly became her client. Vicki started to see him at school and to discuss his behavior with his teachers. She also made me promise that I would contact her in the event of any problems. I was very grateful for this offer, and when things went horribly wrong on the basketball court not long after, I called her for help.

We were thrilled when Dane was selected to play center in the school's basketball team. Rod had shown Dane how to throw balls into a basketball hoop and, providing someone else passed the ball to him, he had developed an exceptional goal-scoring ability. We went to his first match brimming with expectation, ready to cheer him on.

We were so disappointed. Dane simply couldn't understand what was happening around him. This was agonizing for him and for us.

Rod took Dane aside and said, "Dane, you'll have to grab the ball. no one's going to throw it to you. See how the others are doing it?"

Dane was horrified! What was his dad asking him to do? Grabbing the ball contradicted everything he had learned about good manners. He just couldn't understand the rules of the game.

Dane was relegated to the sidelines, and we were thankful for this as we feared a serious confrontation with the other children could take place. Naturally the staff's suggestion that he play again the following week worried us, so we asked Vicki Bitsika to come along. After only a few minutes she agreed with us that, for Dane, competitive team sport was designed for failure. When she spoke to Dane afterward, she said, "Dane, I found that basketball game so confusing! I didn't know which end you were supposed to throw the basket. I even lost track of which team you were in!"

Dane reacted to Vicki's remarks with relief, and he was pleased when she arranged for his withdrawal from the basketball team. Then, very casually, she suggested to Dane that they go tenpin bowling together. Vicki wanted theirs to be a two-way relationship. She felt Dane would respond more positively to her if she developed strong everyday connections with him, rather than if she saw him in a more clinical situation. Before long, Vicki and Dane became friends and bowling partners.

At first Dane found it difficult to discuss his problems with Vicki. However, after a few weeks of tenpin bowling, he was sharing a great deal of his adolescent pain and negativity with her.

Occasionally they'd go bowling with Vicki's two teen-age nieces. Dane always behaved well on these occasions. They'd drive off together chatting away like old friends; they'd play their game and then go for coffee and cake. Vicki coached the girls in how to relate to Dane. She suggested they speak slowly and firmly and enjoy his company. *Hey girls, relax, he's a young guy! Treat him like a young guy.*

Another problem that Vicki helped us deal with at this time was Dane's unorthodox behavior in public. For example, we'd board a tram and a person sitting opposite might offer Dane a brief smile of acknowledgment. On the strength of this smile, Dane would nudge me and declare loudly, "He's my friend, Mum! See, he's smiling at me!"

Then Dane would grimace and stare at his supposed friend until the stranger squirmed with discomfort. He was oblivious to other people's embarrassment, regardless of my admonitions. "Don't stare at people; it's rude," I'd say. "He's not your friend." But my words meant nothing to him.

Then Dane began rushing up and kissing people we'd pause to speak to. Given his difficulties in showing affection, this behavior surprised us. He had seen me occasionally kiss friends I'd meet on the street, so we could only guess that he was mimicking this. He couldn't understand our warnings that, for him, such behavior was inappropriate, and Rod and I began to fear it might result in the gravest consequences. As a handsome thirteen-year-old, Dane was very vulnerable to unwanted attention from strangers.

Vicki Bitsika suggested that a teaching strategy called the "circles concept" be used to help address the problem of Dane's inappropriate behavior. This innovative strategy explains differences in relationships and appropriate degrees of intimacy by placing the student—"me"—in the center of five concentric rings. Closest to "me" is the "hug" circle, followed by "handshake" and "wave." The furthest is "stranger circle, do not touch."

The circles concept worked beautifully for Dane. Within a week or so I could quietly question his response to a stranger. "Have you been introduced, Dane? Is this man in your handshake circle?"

"No, Mum."

"Then he's not your friend, Dane. You don't know him."

"No, Mum, he's not my friend."

And that was the end of Dane's staring at strangers and trying to kiss the wrong people. The circles concept taught him to understand where strangers belonged in his life. He learned why he could wave at certain people even if he hadn't been introduced. He understood that if someone known to him introduces a new person, then that new person moves into Dane's handshake circle.

Some months later I realized just how effectively Dane had embraced the circles concept. A young woman followed us into an elevator. She admired my hair style and asked where I'd had it cut. As I started to answer, Dane nudged me sharply. "Mum, she's not in your handshake circle! She hasn't been introduced!"

By this stage I knew Dane's understanding of the circles concept could accommodate variations, so I said, "No, Dane, I haven't been introduced, but this lady has asked me a question so I will give her my answer."

As Dane became comfortable with the circles concept, we saw him take control of his inner, or "me," circle. He learned that no one else could control this inner circle, just Dane. He felt empowered by this realization, and in turn it gave him a sense of other people's need for space and privacy.

"Are you grumpy, Mum?" he'd ask.

"No, I'm not grumpy," I'd reply. "I'm trying to cook dinner and I need a bit of space."

These answers began to make sense to Dane. I could almost hear him thinking: *This is her space she's talking about. She's busy with dinner. Don't keep intruding.*

This growing comprehension helped to raise Dane's self-esteem. He continues to use and appreciate the circles concept.

Our silver wedding anniversary was coming up and I wanted to do something special for Rod. I wanted to say a big "Thank you" to my patient, loving and long-suffering husband. I can only imagine how hard it must have been for Rod to cope with his challenging job and then to have to come home to more challenges. We would always discuss Dane's day and any problems I'd had before he could share his day with me. We both lived every day with the realization that Dane's needs had to come first. This of course put pressure on our relationship, though I didn't ever feel that our marriage was threatened. We both believed that good marriages are achieved through sheer hard work and determination, and a fundamental regard and respect for each other.

Every now and again I'd arrange a special treat for Rod. Maybe a romantic supper for two on a summer's night, or a glass of port by the fire in winter—be it ever so late in the evening, as we'd never dare interrupt our routine or do anything unexpected at our usual dinnertime. But now, for our silver anniversary, I wanted to do something really special.

When I first saw Rod, he had been riding a motorcycle, a Triumph Thunderbird. At first I hadn't wanted to talk to him—respectable members of the Box Hill younger set like me didn't associate with bikies—but eventually his charm, courteousness and kindness made me forget all my preconceptions.

Rod sold the Thunderbird to pay for our honeymoon and he had never replaced it. He'd always hoped to buy another bike, and sometimes he and I had explored motorcycle showrooms, but for twenty-five years he had placed his own needs last on our list of priorities.

On one of our excursions to the showrooms, I had asked him which bike he would choose if he were to buy one. After careful consideration he indicated a striking bright blue machine. I memorized the bike's make and model number. I worked out that if I sold my stamp collection I could buy this bike for Rod. A stamp and coin dealer I'd once worked for had paid my wages with stamps when he was short of cash, and over the years this collection had become quite valuable.

I bought the bike while Rod was in London on a business trip. It was delivered in a silver-colored vinyl cover, which was fortunate because it saved hours of gift-wrapping! It looked huge in our tiny backyard.

When Rod returned, he spied it rightaway. "Joey!" he cried. "What on earth have you done?"

I whipped the vinyl cover off the machine.

"Happy Silver Anniversary, Rod!"

For the first time in his life, my dear husband was absolutely and utterly at a loss for words. He just gaped in astonishment at his big bright blue Harley-Davidson Super Glide.

The following weekend Rod and I rode "Big Blue" to Violet Town for a celebratory weekend with friends. As we left Melbourne the skies opened up but *we* couldn't turn around and go home. No indeed, not Harley riders! So for the wettest hour and a half that I'll ever remember we followed the white line on the highway through blinding rain, all the way to Violet Town's elegantly restored hotel. There we dined on fine white damask in a private room— after the landlady had stopped laughing and kindly dried our clothes in the hotel's dryer!

Later Rod traded-up "Big Blue" for a black Harley-Davidson softtail custom model. By then he was a foundation member of OZHOG, the Australian chapter of the Harley Owners' Group. Rod became OZHOG's treasurer and, supposedly because he was the only member who could keep track of the money, they dubbed him the "Wizard." Needless to say, his new black Harley-Davidson motorcycle became known as the "Black Wizard."

Rod and I had many wonderful outings with OZHOG and the Black Wizard and eventually Rod began to involve Dane in his love of motorcycles. One day he took him to an OZHOG club-meet where they watched a tattoo competition. Dane was seriously impressed and decided he must have a tattoo too. Rod was worried; he could see himself getting into trouble with me. So he showed Dane the tattoo artist at work with needle and ink. Dane still wanted a tattoo, assuring Rod he wouldn't mind having a needle jabbed into his arm thousands of times!

Rod decided it was time for desperate measures. Back home he sterilized a pin and said to Dane, "Are you sure you want to try this?"

"Yes!"

So Rod jabbed Dane's arm with the pin.

"Did that hurt?"

"YES!"

"Would you like to have hundreds of jabs like that?"

"NO!"

Dane never mentioned tattoos again.

Dane continued to have bouts of deep depression which made him increasingly withdrawn and uncooperative. Rod wondered if their common interest in the motorcycle and Dane's love of rivers could be used to alleviate this depression. He suggested to Dane that they ride the Harley to the Murray River and camp there for the weekend. Dane readily accepted his father's offer.

The weekend, the first time in years that Rod and Dane had spent more than a few hours alone together, was a great success. Rod pitched a tent on a sandy river-bend in an isolated public reserve. Later he described Dane's demeanor as being very peaceful. For two glorious days all his unhappiness appeared to dissipate into the river and the overhanging trees.

Back home, Dane couldn't wait to tell me about his weekend. He wanted me to enjoy this lovely spot too. His pleasure was reflected in his speech and for the first time in many months he appeared alert and untroubled.

The Murray River was such an effective healing agent that within weeks we all headed back there again. We had a wonderful weekend and again Dane was able to put his depression aside, if only for a day or so. We repeated these excursions many times and grew to love this beautiful area. While these camping weekends by the river didn't cure Dane's depression, at least we'd discovered a way to moderate the problem.

With this small victory in place, Rod and I wondered if we could spend a longer vacation beside a river. We decided a houseboat was the answer, and a few weeks later, just before Dane's fourteenth birthday, we were drifting down the river in glorious late autumn weather, admiring the riverbanks from a new perspective.

Dane responded positively to the houseboat's orderly surroundings. It was scrupulously clean and tidy with ample space for passengers to move around. Steering the boat at every opportunity boosted his spirits too; this made him feel useful and grown-up. Most evenings we'd pull ashore and build a small campfire while Dane walked along the riverbank. I believe he enjoyed having this time alone by the river so he could think aloud.

We didn't want that vacation to end, so to snatch an extra day we delayed leaving the river until late Sunday afternoon, and stayed overnight in a motel. After a very early breakfast the next morning, we headed back to Melbourne.

As usual Dane traveled in the back seat. He was singing happily to himself as Rod changed lanes and merged into the freeway's heavy traffic. Suddenly Dane asked if we were going home. His question surprised me. We had discussed our plans, and Rod and I both assumed Dane understood what we were doing.

I said, "Yes, Dane, we're going home now. Dad has to go to work this morning, and I'll take you to school."

In a split second Dane became a screaming, hysterical mess. He beat the car doors and windows with fists and feet and pummeled the seats. He pounded our luggage and threw loose objects around the interior with every ounce of his strength. His shrieks didn't abate for a second. I was terrified. Heaven only knows how Rod managed to control the car in the fast moving freeway traffic.

We had not experienced behavior like this since Dane's childhood. Over the years he had developed many coping skills, and, moreover, had demonstrated clearly that he needed to be at peace with the world, that he wanted to control himself. We hadn't expected to see such an outburst again.

Dane kept on screaming and thrashing and throwing anything he could get his hands on. Desperately I tried to think: Had we overlooked something important? Had we made some dreadful mistake? Somehow Rod managed to drive to a park, hoping the trees would soothe Dane. We half-coaxed and half-dragged him out of the car, groping for words of comfort and reassurance.

But Dane would not be consoled. He just couldn't find a way to regain his composure. The park and the trees didn't help and his screaming and thrashing began to attract attention. We were desperately afraid the police would arrive and take the situation out of our hands. Eventually Dane screamed himself into absolute and utter exhaustion.

The experience devastated us all. The river's gentle gift of peace and tranquillity lay shattered like broken glass. Rod and I searched for answers. We could only conclude that, somehow, we were at fault, that we hadn't explained clearly enough what was going to happen. We resolved that next time we'd do more preparation and role-playing. We'd remember to place past and future events in chronological order. We'd explain what was going to happen one step at a time: *the vacation has finished; now it's time to drive back home; now you'll go back to school.*

Rod and I knew we must identify beginnings and endings for Dane, and never allow an empty space between activities. Perhaps we'd been careless on this occasion. This had to be a one-time incident. Surely he wouldn't lose control again? But he did.

Dane appeared to settle back into his daily routine when we returned. Walking the dog was an important part of this routine and we all enjoyed the long strolls through the parks where the stately trees, expanses of grass and peaceful surroundings met our diverse needs. It was on one of these walks that Dane flew into another paroxysm of violent rage. Again there was absolutely no warning. Screaming with rage, he started beating his clenched fists against a metal road sign. Rod grabbed him in a bear hug, saying, "What's this? What's the problem?" but Dane kept on screaming and lashing out. It was only Rod's physical strength that eventually constrained his son's frenzy. Exhausted, we turned for home. Then we realized how many metal road signs stood between us and our front door.

Dane broke loose from his father's clutches and rushed at each and every metal road sign on the way home, screaming and lashing out with his fists. He was like a violent stranger. He even looked different in that fearful state. How could we help him? Was this the result of adolescent turmoil or something much worse? We just didn't know.

Weeks later, during another walk, Dane began "badmouthing" nothing in particular, in a very loud voice. Inevitably he'd learned to swear from his classmates at school but he understood these were bad words that must not be used in public or at home.

On this particular day he must have been feeling particularly bad so he used each and every bad word he knew at full volume.

Calmly Rod admonished him. "Not in public, Dane. You don't swear in front of ladies."

Dane's response was to scoop up a handful of gravel from the road and throw it at a passing car. Then he completely lost control, screaming, kicking and lashing out at everything within reach. Jaeger was terrified. I remember grabbing her as a man hurried from a nearby house to stare at us.

Rod took Dane by the shoulders and forced him to the footpath. He then kneeled astride his son, placing his arms on each side of Dane's body as if to shelter and calm him without making actual contact. The screams persisted but Dane didn't resist Rod's efforts. I could see that Rod was adapting the "quiet room" techniques we'd learned years ago when Dane was at Irabina.

Assuming I was an onlooker, a passing jogger suggested he phone the police. Heaven forbid! The assertiveness in my voice when I replied startled me. "I can't explain this to you, so please let them be. We're doing our best." The jogger moved on and the man from the house silently withdrew.

When Dane's screams eventually eased, Rod moved his arms aside, very slightly. The instant the screaming stopped altogether, Rod gave him a light, non-intrusive hug, like we'd used in the quiet room. He was then able to get Dane back onto his feet and, struggling with him each and every step of the way, we headed for home.

Rod had always yearned to have a normal, loving father–son relationship with Dane, but he could never reach him on this level. Then, very suddenly, after the last of these terrible outbursts, something changed. Dane began to make it clear that he needed his dad, that he wanted to include him in his day-to-day activities. "Dad, can we go for a ride?" he'd ask, or "Dad, can we go to the park?"

Out of the depths of Dane's sorrow, father and son finally made emotional contact. By giving Dane his physical and emotional support during those terrible times, Rod was able to move beyond his role of cycling and swimming teacher to that of friend.

Apart from the immediate family and very close friends, there was little support for Rod as the father of a child with special needs. At social or business functions he was seldom questioned about Dane. It was as if by ignoring Dane's existence the "problem" would disappear and Rod felt this deeply: "My kid wasn't playing football or soccer or basket-ball or cricket. My kid wasn't a junior athlete at the state school. My kid wasn't even going to the state school! We never attended my employer's "family picnics." I couldn't reconcile my role as an executive with that of father of a child whose behavior was so different. I couldn't cope with the pressure and I guess that wasn't terribly courageous of me."

However, with the sorrow came the joy. "My son's melancholy is beyond my comprehension, but for a person who must learn every emotion and experience he has the great ability to teach the learned immense knowledge. The crushing weight of having an impaired child does not diminish with time, but Dane makes me stronger to bear it."

Dane's outbursts were terrifying. Rod and I had no idea what we were dealing with. His medication, which had helped in the past, didn't seem to be working, so we sought help. With Dr. John having moved, we obtained a referral to another psychiatrist.

Dane had developed the ability to appear calm in the midst of a tantrum. He perfected this technique for doctors' appointments; he knew that if he calmed himself and behaved politely, he'd be out of there faster. Then he'd break into another tantrum in the elevator or out on the street.

This ability made it impossible for me to explain the magnitude of our problems to the new psychiatrist. He listened to what I had to say, but saw nothing but good manners and calm behavior from Dane. I believe it was only to placate me that the psychiatrist suggested we "play around" with medication.

The results of this medication were negligible. The psychiatrist's fees were outrageous and we didn't appear to be getting anywhere, but despite this we persevered with regular consultations. Then, some weeks later, Dane threw a tantrum in the car outside the consulting rooms. I asked the psychiatrist to help me get Dane out of the car. He was astonished to see Dane completely out of control. When he asked how long this sort of behavior had been going on, I replied, "This is exactly why we are coming to see you!"

Somewhat chastened, the psychiatrist began to give Dane a series of tests. During each appointment they'd disappear behind closed doors while I waited outside. Afterward I'd ask Dane, "How do you feel about this doctor? Is he helping you to keep your control?" but Dane was always non-committal.

One day the psychiatrist took me aside. He said it was time for us to have a serious discussion and that Rod should join us. For the third time in Dane's life, we heard that dreaded phrase "placed into care."

According to this psychiatrist Dane was beyond help and should be protected from his own self-destructive behavior. He suggested we place him in a rural institution, describing it like some sort of vacation resort. "It's so lovely!" he enthused. "It's near the mountains with a river nearby. He'll be happy there."

The psychiatrist's words were painful and cut us deeply, but this time we didn't even bother to argue. We knew all about these lovely places. We'd ignored such advice before and we'd survived. We'd ignore it again, but could we survive this time?

Some time later Dane said to me, "We don't have to go back to that doctor, do we?"

"No, we don't have to go back."

"That's good!" Dane exclaimed.

This surprised me. "Why is it good, Dane?"

Dane replied, "That was silly. He made me sit in a baby chair. He made me play with a doll's house. Dane's not a baby!"

Dane still lacked the confidence to express an opinion without being asked. He needed me to ask him why it was good that we weren't going back. He needed my "permission" before he could express his own feelings about those costly and wasteful appointments. He also couldn't talk about his problems. He'd act out his frustrations and anxieties. And his need for sameness remained very strong. He'd resist all new information and communicated this resistance with body language, not with speech. Any failure to prepare Dane for a new situation, through simplified role-playing for example, still invited mayhem. He suffered, we suffered and everyone around us suffered.

These preparation skills were unexpectedly reinforced by three three-day speech camps Dane attended. They were conducted as practical work experience for speech pathology students from La Trobe University in conjunction with the Autistic Family Support Association (AFSA). The students observed and interacted with the children in natural, fun situations such as rope climbing, playing on a flying fox and exploring bushland. In this way they were able to assess the children's motor, vocabulary and language skills. There were also information sessions for the parents where we learned practical skills about role-playing and non-stressful family discussion, and how we could help improve Dane's comprehension, his one-to-one communication skills and his vocabulary.

For Dane and for us, these family discussions became immensely valuable. Dane grew to accept them as the best way to introduce new areas of interest, discuss problems and resolve conflicts. They became a mechanism for improving his communication skills, and for helping him prepare for new and different situations. Eventually he became accustomed to having open discussions in other settings, with other groups of people.

In these family discussions, to accommodate Dane's need for sameness, we always followed exactly the same "agenda." I'd speak first, then Rod, then Dane, then me again, and so on. Nobody could interrupt or speak out of turn.

To this day, family discussion remains an essential part of our routine. Dane has learned to ask for a family discussion whenever he wants to introduce a new activity into his life or to gauge our feelings on a particular subject. He sees it as a friendly coming together without pressure. If problems arise, he'll often be the first to suggest we have a family discussion. We still use family discussions to reinforce our everyday schedules and to work out our future plans. It has also become a tool for helping Dane consider other people's needs.

The speech camp sessions honed our role-playing skills too, reinforcing our opinion that it was easier for Dane to mimic our behavior than to understand our words. We learned how role-playing diverted the emphasis from Dane and removed the pressure. To mimic was fun! And then, when it became time to do the real thing, it was as though he thought: *I've done this once, so I've already taken the risk. Now I can do it again.*

Role-playing helped us draw Dane into society. He'd always been on the fringe. He didn't understand his role within the family or the neighborhood or school. Now role-playing helped him to understand how he fit into these areas and to answer questions like *Who am I?* and *Where do I belong?*

Dane had responded well to using the speech camp's computers, so he was invited to attend weekly computer training at La Trobe University's Lincoln Institute. We bought a home computer with identical software packages to reinforce those sessions.

This was very successful. Dane was soon adding, subtracting and multiplying with the contents of our fruit bowl; learning to tell the time by creating his own timepieces on the computer screen; and playing with the reading and spelling programs for hours on end. He enjoyed pitting himself against the computer. It provided an acceptable and non-threatening challenge, and he knew there was more to come if he completed each exercise to the best of his ability.

It was difficult for Dane's teachers to show him how to do these things at school. He interpreted all teaching efforts as intrusions into his space, but the main problem was that he couldn't understand verbal instructions, and so became bored and restless. The computer screen's immediate and visual response provided an ideal teaching aid.

Those three camps and his subsequent visits to the Lincoln Institute were a highlight of Dane's early teenage years. For me, they offered invaluable guidance and hope for the future, especially the hope that Dane would one day be able to relate to others. I felt he was beginning to do this, so I was very happy for him when he was invited to one of his teenage cousin's birthday parties. I could never have anticipated the emotional impact this party would have on me.

Dane's behavioral differences were not as apparent at school and the speech camps, but as I watched him at that party, the huge emotional and developmental gap between my son and his cousins was very obvious.

The pain of this recognition surprised me. I had watched him with his cousins for years, so why was this hurt so intense? Later I confided in a friend whose daughter also has an intellectual disability. "My God, my son really does have a pervasive developmental disorder! It's never going to go away!"

My friend agreed with me, adding, "You're still grieving, Junee."

I was surprised. I thought I had worked through my grieving for Dane but my friend was absolutely right. Would I ever stop grieving for my child, I wondered.

What's a rainbow?

Dane was searching for a purpose to his life. He didn't understand why he was at school, and this uncertainty clouded his life. One day Vicki Bitsika told us that a two-week work experience position was about to become available at the Victoria College cafeteria, affectionately known as "the Caf," and she suggested that Dane take it. Rod and I were astonished. Work experience? For Dane? How on earth could this be done? Someone like Dane doesn't simply walk into a new situation and do work experience.

Vicki assured us that Dane would receive ample preparation from an Alpha Terrace staff member, and that this same staff member would remain by his side the first two weeks at the Caf. So Rod and I agreed Dane should do the work experience.

For almost eight weeks, Dane worked with Shelley O'Connell, the Alpha Terrace staff member, at Bulleen and, occasionally, at home. Wisely, Shelley didn't expect an immediate welcome from Dane. She understood the stress that a new person and a new routine in his life could cause. She sewed an apron to his measurements and together they fabric-painted this with Dane's name, colorful logos, flowers and abstract forms. They had fun together and the apron was Dane's visual clue that Shelley was his new friend.

Dane needed encouragement to become more expansive, so Shelley worked on his observation and comprehension skills. For example, she asked him to examine Snoopy and the Peanuts cartoons. Then she would ask him questions: *Can a dog really ice skate? Have you been ice skating? Are they wearing summer or winter clothes?* In this way, she encouraged Dane not to just look at the cartoons but to analyze them as well. She used this technique to sharpen his awareness of items he'd handle at the Caf: apples, bananas, knives, bread and so on.

Through her outstanding teaching skills, Shelley developed a wonderful rapport with Dane. Whereas I'd failed to raise his enthusiasm for anything more than stirring and mixing, she soon had him slicing tomatoes, washing and shredding salad, grating vegetables and wiping benches. He'd help me cheerfully and effectively in the kitchen and then he'd go out and help Rod with the barbecue!

Shelley talked to Dane about all those questions he was likely to be asked when he was at the Caf and encouraged him to consider his answers. *Where do you go to school? When did you start work experience? How old are you? Where do you live?* She also asked him to write down the list of tasks he would have to perform. This was *Dane's* list for *Dane's* work experience in *Dane's* printing—it gave him ownership of the things he'd do at the Caf. The "List" worked beautifully and years later this simple concept would play another very important part in Dane's life.

Since childhood, Dane has responded to photographs of familiar places and friends. Shelley used photos of the building, the staff and the grounds to turn the Caf into a reality for him. She also compiled a daily timetable listing his co-workers names, the names of the people he would have lunch with, who would collect him after work, and so on. She covered every angle in order to limit his exposure to the unexpected.

Snapshots of a young boy growing up

Dane (nine months) and Rod.

"Smile for the camera."

Dane in the pool at Irabina Autistic Centre with Bill McCallum and friend Darren.

Dane and Jennifer Emery-Smith at Dane's fifth birthday party.

Balloons were for special occasions.

Dane's baptism.

Dane's sixth birthday and the start of his cycling career.

Gypsy caravan
vacation with Blackie,
a gentle Clydesdale.

Rod and Dane on a
houseboat on the Murray
River.

Performing at his parents' 26th anniversary party with music therapist Anja Tait.

Dane at 14 helped out in the kitchen at Warrawong Day Care Kindergarten.

Dancing with Erin Young, Dane celebrated his 14th birthday.

Dane and his Fijian friends on Matagi Island.

Dane's Paris vacation, visiting with Angolan Cluny Sisters at the Mother House.

Winning his weight division at
a powerlifting competition.

Dane with Ray Ryan at
the end of the City to
Surf Run.

Friends from the gym gave
Dane a large copy of this
photo for his 21st birthday.

Dane proudly displays his gold and silver medals
for State Ten Pin Bowling Special Olympics.

Rod, Junee and Dane.

But the unexpected seems to pop up anyway. Everything appeared to be in place for Dane's work experience when a crisis at Alpha Terrace made Shelley unavailable to be his support co-worker.

We felt overwhelming disappointment. It would be impossible to assign an unfamiliar support person at this late stage. Then Vicki Bitsika came to the rescue. As she worked as a consultant with the Alpha Terrace outreach program, her "hands-on" experiences were limited. The idea of working as Dane's support person greatly appealed to her.

Dane's progress at the Caf surpassed all our expectations. With Vicki discreetly nearby, he helped with food preparation, sorted cutlery, collected dishes, wiped tables, washed dishes and emptied bins. His first task each day was the buttering of endless bread rolls. While the repetition appealed to Dane, this was an experience Vicki hadn't anticipated!

The Caf's strict daily routine appeared to reduce Dane's on-going fear of change between one activity and the next. The list of tasks also played a useful role here.

The Caf was a wonderful experience for Dane. He thoroughly enjoyed all the tasks and it changed his self-image. He knew he could function as an individual, outside the confines of home and a special school. It gave schoolwork new meaning too. Now he'd say, "If I go to school, then I can get a job!"

Working at the Caf had a profound effect on Vicki Bitsika too. She later wrote about how her time with Dane changed her philosophy and guidelines for working with people with autism:

Before the Caf experience I believed my prime function was to change the person's behavior through research-based strategies. After the Caf I became convinced that any treatment or intervention needed to come from the professional having developed a relationship with the

client. This shift in my thinking came at a time
when the literature told us that people with autism
were "aloof," and "lacked empathy," and had
minimal interest in developing relationships with
others.

Dane's responses during the Caf experience gave
me the confidence to say, "This is what Dane and I do.
These are the approaches I use with Dane." I'd hear
cynical remarks from some of my colleagues about
"touchy feely stuff with a kid that doesn't even
understand" but I'd recognized that children with
autism need the option of talking to a professional
person about their feelings and experiences, and putting
these into some meaningful context . . . The lessons I
learned buttering endless pieces of bread with Dane
guide my professional practice to this day.

The success of Dane's hand-written task list helped us
to recognize and deal with his all-consuming need to know
exactly what was going to happen next. This didn't relate to a
preference for one activity over another, but rather to his fear
of the unplanned space between each activity. By age
fourteen, this fear became so intense that he needed to know
what we'd be doing each and every second of the day. To
suggest we'd do something in five minutes, or even one minute,
was enough to provoke a tantrum. We had to account for
those intervening seconds.

For example, we'd outline our plans for Saturday morning. "We'll have breakfast, Dane, then we'll go shopping, then
we'll have coffee, then we'll ride our bikes to the park, and
then we'll have lunch."

Suddenly our pleasant ride through the park would be
interrupted by Dane's booming voice. "What are we going to
do when we get home?"

I'd reply, "Dane, we've only just started our ride! But you can help Dad put the bicycles away when we get home, and then we'll have lunch."

This wouldn't satisfy him. "What can I do before lunch is ready?"

"You can wash your hands."

These questions would continue unrelentingly throughout the ride. There'd be no let-up, and the sheer intensity of his demands began to frighten us.

Dane disliked recess and lunchtime at school for the same reason: the fear of the void. Nervously he would wander around, unable to relate to anything or anyone in this unstructured situation. He'd become overwrought and back in the classroom he'd be unable to focus on his lessons.

Rod and I suggested he use the computer room during recess and lunchtime. This solved the problem. Dane enjoyed computers and now he knew exactly what he'd be doing each and every recess and lunchtime.

Weekends in the country continued to help with Dane's depression, and in winter, when riverside camping wasn't comfortable, we borrowed a country cottage. Kiely-Lynn Waters, the daughter of our friends in Bega, was studying in Melbourne, and we invited her to join us on one of these weekends.

We felt very special as we cruised down the freeway with Jaeger, Dane and Kiely-Lynn in the back seat, a basket of food in the trunk, the stereo playing and the dashboard lights blinking and flashing and making clever calculations about our fuel consumption. Rod had just taken delivery of a brand new car, only the second of its make and model to roll off the Australian assembly line. It was equipped with every last little device the computer designers could create.

Suddenly the music stopped, the flashing lights faded and this marvel of technology rolled to a standstill. We didn't have a mobile phone then so Rod hitched a ride to a nearby town.

As far as Dane was concerned, we were on our way to Labertouche. We weren't supposed to be sitting beside a freeway in the middle of nowhere! Quietly Kiely-Lynn took control. She chatted to Dane about his music, and school, and Jaeger, and her home at Bega. They walked Jaeger beside the freeway, then they talked some more. Kiely-Lynn speaks quietly. She's precise in her speech and literal in her choice of words; she doesn't use colloquialisms such as "sock it to me" which would send Dane hunting for a sock to give her. She told Dane about her own activities on the assumption that he'd be interested, as any friend would be. Her approach was genuine. For years, Dane called Kiely-Lynn his "sister."

After many hours and many questions from Dane, Rod appeared in a little old Toyota Corolla, the only car rental he could get. There was scarcely room for us, let alone all our provisions for a weekend that was fast disappearing!

It was almost dark by the time we arrived at the cottage. I could see Kiely-Lynn was tired so I suggested she relax while I unpacked our dinner. I forgot to warn her about the Labertouche lizards. Seconds later a dreadful shriek shattered the tranquillity as she chose to share the resident lizards' sofa. Yes, these were *real* lounge lizards! They had the house to themselves all week so who were we humans to interfere?

We had many more happy excursions to Labertouche with Kiely-Lynn. Then, at the end of her semester, I drove her to the bus terminal to catch a bus home for her vacation. Dane came with us, and his reaction when he realized she was leaving Melbourne was amazing. He really didn't want her to go. As the bus pulled away he ran alongside, begging his "sister" to stay.

This was exceptional behavior for a young person with autism. In those years the media promoted the theory that people with autism were devoid of all emotion. Dane's obvious distress at the bus terminal made me wonder about those theories. Would he have chased Kiely-Lynn's bus if they were true?

After a brief period of calm Dane had yet another dreadful outburst. This time, Rod wasn't on hand to support his son. It happened just before Christmas, when Dane was fourteen and a half. Margaret had joined us for a day in the city. Dane had enjoyed the traditional storybook theme of the Myers Christmas window decorations in previous years, so around mid-afternoon we entered the crowded mall to look at the displays. As we moved toward the first window, I was vaguely aware of someone gently bumping Dane's arm.

After a day in the city, and in that dense crowd, just one little bump was too much for Dane. He threw his arms into the air and screamed at the top of his voice. He screamed and screamed and pounded that huge store window as though he wanted to smash it to smithereens.

As I tried to gather my wits I glanced at Margaret. In those few seconds my friend's face became a mirror in which I was compelled to look. I saw on her face, and in her body language, the same feelings I'd experienced so many times. She was frozen with shock. She'd shared our problems for a very long time but had never witnessed anything like this. Should I deal with Margaret or with Dane? His frenzied pounding left me no choice—I couldn't begin to imagine the replacement cost of that window.

The crowd backed off in alarm, leaving a space around us for which I was grateful, and I prayed nobody would try to "help." I knew we couldn't go into the store—that would only make matters worse—and then I remembered a three-sided nook at the end of the GPO's veranda where I'd occasionally sought shelter on wet days. Maybe we could hide there.

Margaret followed my lead and together we shielded Dane with our arms, taking great care not to touch him. Very slowly we walked him, still screaming and lashing about, through the crowd and down the mall toward the steps. Slowly and painfully we coaxed him up one step, then another, then another, trying to reassure nervous onlookers at each step. Eventually we negotiated each of those eight steps and reached the three-sided enclosure.

For ten minutes, or maybe even longer, Dane screamed and hammered the stone walls while Margaret and I guarded this improvised quiet room. I knew it was pointless talking to him and I prayed we'd be left alone.

Eventually the tantrum eased and I did my best to echo the quiet room routine. "Oh, Dane," I said, "you must be feeling so much better. You are in control now, Dane."

He replied, "Yes, Mum." Then he said, "I think we'll give the Myers windows a miss, Mum."

Readily Margaret and I agreed.

Then he said, "Can we have our coffee now, Mum?"

I replied, "Yes Dane, but I have an awful headache. Let's find a quiet coffee shop."

Experiencing her beloved godson at his very worst came as a terrible shock to Margaret. But at least it had shown her that without interference from other people, and given time and correct handling, Dane had learned to eventually take control of his own outbursts.

Despite these outbursts I persisted in trying to expand Dane's interests. Brunswick's proximity to the city helped me acquaint him with live music and theater. I hoped a live performance of *The Wind in the Willows* in the Melbourne Botanical Gardens would be a good introduction to theater. He wouldn't be crowded and if necessary we could leave without a disturbance.

The Wind in the Willows proved a great choice. There were no seats where Dane had to sit, and no forbidden areas. We joined a young audience following the characters around a lake, under shrubs and up trees, and Dane loved it.

We moved on to performances for children at the Royal Melbourne Institute of Technology. Then Rod and I prepared him for *Cats* and *Starlight Express* with theater programs and audio tapes. Dane enjoyed these productions—lots of singing and dancing and not much talking! Then we took him to rock concerts with Pink Floyd and Simply Red. I'm not sure who learned most—Dane, Rod or myself!

Movies were less successful. There were too many distractions for Dane. One day we took him to see *E.T.* For the first half-hour or so he repeatedly asked to go to the toilet, so Rod suggested a walk while I watched the movie.

Afterward I expressed my disappointment to Dane. "I'm sorry you didn't see the movie. I thought you'd enjoy it. E.T. was so cute!"

Dane replied forcefully, "E.T. was not a cute little fellow. I did not like E.T.!" For Dane, who characteristically spoke in a monotone, this forcefulness was unusually expressive.

Dane loved music so we wondered if he would enjoy playing an instrument. I contacted the Music Therapists' Association, who put me in touch with Anja Tait.

Anja introduced Dane to music in a wonderful, nonstressful way. She had a soothing nature and laughter in her voice. She based her approach on an awareness of Dane's interests and strengths. She collected instruments from around the world and, as she played them, she'd tell Dane about each instrument's country of origin, its people and its culture. Dane was fascinated. Through music Anja offered him knowledge and experiences that enhanced his self-expression and his self-esteem.

Together they wrote a song to articulate his depression, though there was never a hint of depression when Anja was around. They made music in a rowing boat on the Yarra River, and chatted with passing oarsmen. They played a grand piano in a music store and explored the listening booths.

Dane learned how to choose a CD and ask for it to be played. Anja introduced him to opera and ballet, and to the Melbourne Symphony Orchestra where they met the musicians in the orchestra pit at intermission.

Dane always remembers special occasions and with Anja he prepared a very special treat for our twenty-sixth wedding anniversary. It was truly a memorable evening.

Dane's eyes sparkled with excitement as he proudly presented each guest with a printed program, beautifully decorated with autumn leaves. At Dane's request we had dressed formally, and he wore the traditional performing colors of black and white. He played a tune on the double bass and the lute. He sang a duet with Anja, and then accompanied her with cymbals while she played a number of instruments. As we applauded the final selection, Dane took three deep bows, then finished the concert with a little speech.

Rod and I couldn't have had a more wonderful anniversary gift.

Some years earlier, I had given Dane a picture book called *Annie's Rainbow* for his birthday. At the time I hadn't realized how much its one-dimensional illustrations done in subdued colors would appeal to him. As I read and re-read the story, he'd examine the diminutive figure of little Annie negotiating pathways through mysterious, forbidding forests, the pictures having no shadows or perspective and brightened only by her rainbow. Dane could examine the simple illustrations without becoming confused and thus could concentrate on the story.

On a vacation not long after, there were showers of rain each afternoon, followed by spectacular rainbows when the sun broke through. Dane would gasp with delight, "Look, Mum. There's Annie's rainbow!" Now he had a new interest in his life. Rainbows!

One evening, just before his fifteenth birthday, Dane and I were watching a glorious rainbow arching over the Melbourne skyline.

"What's a rainbow, Mum?" he asked me.

I couldn't bring myself to explain all that business of refracted light, so I said, "Well, Dane, I believe rainbows are God's way of saying he loves us."

We stood quietly together, watching the rainbow. Then my son turned toward me and looked deeply into my eyes.

"I love you, too, Mum!" he said.

For the first time in his life, I knew my son really did love me.

An excellent driver

Today, whenever Dane hears of a boy turning fifteen, he'll exclaim, "I feel sorry for him." We struggled too, as Dane confronted the frustration and anger that accompanies so many young men through puberty.

As a child, Dane just existed. Apart from his tantrums, there were no feelings attached to his words or expressions, he didn't seem to experience any emotions, and he had no apparent understanding of happiness or sadness. Now his body was changing, he was beginning to experience emotion, and it was all way beyond his comprehension. On top of this, he couldn't just go and kick a football or hang out with his peers like other teenagers experiencing the turmoils of adolescence. We had to decide whether he'd ride his bike, take Jaeger for a walk, or do something else. We had to work out what he'd do each and every moment of the day, and with these constraints he just couldn't express his perfectly normal frustrations and anxieties.

Eventually all this pent-up emotion exploded. One day he lifted up our garden bench and, screaming with anguish, he pounded it into the brick-paved courtyard until it smashed into splinters.

I dropped to my knees in utter despair. I wasn't praying. I just dropped. I remember crying out loud, "Isn't there anyone who can help us?"

Immediately Dane stopped his atrocious behavior. He put his hand on my shoulder and looked into my eyes. Then he said, "Isn't there, Mum? Isn't there anyone who can help us?" He wasn't just repeating my words. Then, for the first time in his life, my son reached out and hugged me.

Out of that unspeakable misery we finally made a two-way connection. And I believe that at that moment he was the only person alive who really understood how I felt.

We might not have survived that year without Vicki Bitsika. Time and time again she helped us to understand how Dane detested being out of control, why he couldn't help himself and how, at long last, he really needed us. Constantly we'd say to him, "We disagree with your behavior, Dane, but we love you."

Dane had been seeing Vicki for counseling for around two years now. After he pulverized our garden bench she offered extra support, and we arranged that I'd phone her when this became necessary. Between his screaming and thrashing, I'd hold the receiver to his ear. When he heard Vicki's voice, he'd pause and slowly take the receiver. Then he'd talk to her. As his voice softened and his eyes cleared, we'd hear him say, "Yes Vicki. That's right, Vicki."

Vicki used the telephone as a tool to deal with Dane's on-going fear of change. She was giving him permission to change his behavior. He didn't understand that he could use his own thoughts to change his tantrums. If a tantrum developed in the house, for example, he believed that he was powerless to abandon that bad mood for as long as he stayed in the house.

Vicki's voice took him away, via the telephone, from the scene of his tantrum, away from the place where he'd fallen into the bad mood. If Vicki was unavailable, I'd phone Rod or Margaret. Hearing their familiar voices insisting "You can take control, Dane; you can change" helped him overcome his fear of making that change. To this day a telephone conversation with Margaret will deflect an onset of anxiety.

Vicki Bitsika became our lifeline and Dane always looked forward to her counseling sessions. They'd begin by discussing their activities and this allowed Vicki to identify his immediate needs. Using a pencil she'd write down the relevant information: "I rode my bicycle to Princes Park. The boys yelled at me. Vicki went to the beach." Dane would overwrite her words, thus giving him ownership of the information.

Then Vicki would raise matters relating to his activities: "What could we do when the boys yell in Princes Park? What coping mechanisms could we use? How does Vicki deal with rude people at the beach?" By talking about her own experiences, Vicki preserved Dane's dignity. She also did this by obtaining his permission to read the diary she encouraged him to keep, and by obtaining his permission to share his confidences with me. Vicki always focused on developing Dane's self-esteem.

Vicki explained to us the coping mechanisms she taught to Dane. We introduced them at home and gradually we were also able to help him control his bad moods. If he began to slide we'd say, "What did Vicki suggest you do in this situation?" We knew the answer but it had to come from him.

I vividly remember the first time I helped Dane avoid a tantrum on the street. A stranger accidentally bumped him. Before he could vocalize his obvious displeasure and look for a hard surface to bang his clenched fist on, I very quickly asked, "Dane, what has Vicki suggested? Talk to me about it!"

"Talking about it" was one of Vicki's coping mechanisms.

Dane replied, "That man shouldn't have bumped me, Mum."

I said, "That was an accident, Dane."

Dane looked at me in astonishment. "I've controlled my temper!" he gasped.

Now Dane knew he could control his bad temper himself. Like everything else, once Dane has learned something he'll remember it always.

Although we had learned to steer Dane away from a tantrum, we couldn't be permanently at his side redirecting his moods like traffic police. He had to learn to do this for himself, so Vicki began to "withdraw" from these situations. "Dane," she'd say, "you can use your own control. You can do it on your own."

The telephone was a good distancing strategy. While it provided a bridge between Dane and Vicki, at the same time it made him take more responsibility for himself. As he gradually learned to apply his control mechanisms on his own, the telephone became a secondary tool.

Using "talk" as a coping mechanism encouraged Dane to open up to the subject of autism. One day he glanced at a television documentary I was watching. On the screen was a group of around thirty people with disabilities. Immediately Dane exclaimed, "Look, Mum, that man's autistic!" He pointed to a middle-aged man flapping his hands and rocking gently backward and forward. From that sizeable group of people he picked one person with autistic characteristics in a split second.

Then he said, "Isn't it sad, Mum? That man didn't go to Irabina."

I was astonished and gratified that Dane could so accurately and immediately identify the man with autism, and that he'd choose to speak about this to me. This was the first time Dane had used the word "autistic."

The list of treatment programs for children with autism is seemingly endless. It ranges from "miracle cures" (mostly unavailable in Australia) to vitamin therapy and intensive training requiring teams of assistants to work with the child for hours each day.

Rod and I investigated and agonized over many of these programs. Would this treatment or that be right for Dane, and should we subject him to the trauma of overseas travel or to the intensity of prolonged "training" sessions? We'd always find ourselves asking the same question. Would this help him to be happy? That's all we've ever really wanted for our son—just to be happy.

I discussed these issues at length with Vicki Bitsika. She always referred to the lack of scientific proof that any single treatment or program is appropriate for all children with autism. Vicki maintained that to be truly effective any treatment had to result in a better quality of life for the child both immediately and in the long term. She interpreted quality of life as being the child's capacity for independent functioning, extracting meaning from the environment and remaining calm during demanding situations. To achieve this better quality of life for Dane, we believed we must first consider the physical and emotional needs of the whole family. Thus we decided not to try these programs, and Vicki supported us in this decision.

A trip to Corowa on the Harley with Rod introduced another passionate interest into Dane's life—mobile homes. He and Rod stayed overnight in a mobile home park. Rod sent Dane off to the park office to fetch cooking utensils; this made Dane feel important and set the scene for a happy weekend. He was very impressed with their mobile home. He appreciated the clearly defined parameters of its uncluttered space. It was so neat and clean!

Shortly after the Corowa trip, Dane experienced his first plane flight. Well prepared for this through role-playing, he traveled alone to Bega to spend a short vacation with our friends Llewyn and Greer Waters. On his return, we naturally expected to hear all about the plane but, no, he had far more exciting news. He'd stayed in a mobile home!

At Dane's request, Llewyn and Greer had booked two nights in a vacation trailer at Tathra Beach, only fifteen minutes' drive from their own, very comfortable, home. Greer assured me they'd all had a great time. She also told me how, when Dane found a broom, she suggested he might enjoy sweeping away the few cobwebs on the outside walls of their home. Before Greer realized what was happening, Dane had cleaned down every home in the park.

Before Dane's visit to Tathra, we had enjoyed regular Sunday drives to the beach or to the mountains. Now Dane began begging to visit mobile-home showrooms. From the day he explored his first mobile-home display these became an obsession, but a productive one. He was soon identifying trailer makes and models on the freeway. His very genuine interest in mobile homes provided opportunities for us to expand his language skills and interaction with other people.

He became calm in these places. Everything was predictable: refrigerators, stoves, bunks, tables and cup-boards were all found in each unit. Dane found this sameness comforting. It reflected the orderly way he liked to live: a place for everything and everything in its place. If Rod and I had to visit yet another mobile-home outlet to reach this state of bliss then so be it! I'm certain we met every sales-person in Melbourne. They must have wondered about us.

At fifteen, Dane's states of bliss were few and far between. He was outgrowing Bulleen Special School and beginning to realize that some other young men didn't live at home. He began to see leaving home as an instant cure for his woes and became very assertive in his insistence that this happen quickly. These new tantrums where Dane demanded to leave home were crushing for Rod and me.

What could we do? With most educational and residential facilities totally inappropriate for Dane's needs, our options were very limited. I spent hours each day making fruitless phone calls, and Dane became increasingly difficult.

This new challenge coincided with a pronounced shift in government philosophy. After a century of ignoring clients' wishes, government directives turned around to: *Let's interview the client, and hear what the client wants.* In response to my innumerable calls, a government representative visited our home to interview Dane.

"What do you want, Dane?" she asked him. "You don't want to be at home, so where would you like to live?"

She wrote copious notes as the interview dragged on. After an hour of this I interrupted by offering her tea.

Dane announced, "This lady says I can live wherever I want to live, Mum! She's going to find me a place to live!"

Silently, I wished her good luck.

After more questions she said, "Well, there might be a vacancy at Broadmeadows."

"I don't want to live at Broadmeadows!" Dane almost shouted.

"But Dane, you might like it when you see the house."

No, Dane wouldn't like it and, no, he didn't want to see the house. For the umpteenth time I heard the interviewer ask, "Well, Dane, where would you like to live?"

Then Dane had a bright idea. "Oh, I know!" he exclaimed. "In a mobile home! Near the Murray River! That's where I want to live, thank you!"

This interview created months of unnecessary conflict and distress for us all. Dane rejected our explanations about why he couldn't live in a mobile home beside the Murray River. Over and over he would repeat, "That lady said I can live anywhere I like!"

The time had arrived for Dane to leave Bulleen Special School. As he was so desperate to leave home, I tried to find a residential educational facility for him but this was easier said than done. I spent weeks searching. Eventually Rod and I were amazed to discover Churinga, a weekly boarding school, ôperated by the St. John of God Brothers, for young people with an intellectual disability. I'd spent countless hours on the phone and traipsing around government department offices and yet no one had mentioned this place.

Churinga had modern brick buildings, landscaped grounds, excellent recreational facilities and clean, comfortable dormitories. Rod and I were impressed with the standard of work displayed in the classrooms, and as well the school supplemented regular lessons with work-experience placements. Here Dane would be helped to move into the wider world.

Dane was impressed with Churinga too. "Are they going to let me live here and go to school?" he asked. "When can I come?" He sounded so enthusiastic we were delighted.

Preparing Dane effectively for Churinga was difficult, as we couldn't anticipate the daily routine there. But despite slight reservations, Dane remained eager and happy to begin his first term at Churinga. We dropped him off full of high expectations and looked forward to his homecoming the following weekend.

Our hopes were dashed when we picked him up. His mood was belligerent and this persisted for months. We did our best to flow with his difficult and draining behavior, and put it down to the change from Bulleen. On his weekends at home, Dane couldn't cope with even the briefest lapse in our activities. Now, more than ever, he needed to know what we were doing next, and after that, and after that. So, to keep the peace, we began to cram our weekends with activities. The problem diminished as we developed our own coping skills, yet a shadow loomed over each and every weekend.

Churinga was attractively situated in semi-rural country-side in Greensborough, on Melbourne's north-eastern outskirts. Once again we faced the prospect of long drives between school and home and yet how pleasant life would have been had distance been our only concern. On Sunday evenings, Dane would use all his manipulation skills to postpone his return to school. His demeanor improved once Rod coaxed him into the car and he appeared to enjoy the actual drive. Then, as they drove through Churinga's front gates, Dane would break down.

Each and every Sunday evening, Rod could only watch helplessly as Dane cried, screamed and tore at his clothing, his facial expressions so contorted he was almost unrecognizable. I'd send Dane back to school as neat as a pin and by the time they reached Churinga's front door he'd be utterly dishevelled. It was devastating for Rod to have to apologize for his son's shredded clothes and missing buttons.

It wasn't that Dane disliked Churinga. He made friends and the teachers were wonderful. On a number of occasions we drove out to the school where, unobserved by Dane, we watched him interacting with the other young people. We saw our son chasing balls and running and jostling and behaving like any other happy fifteen-year-old. He certainly didn't appear to be unhappy.

And yet the pain of those Sunday nights became almost unbearable. Rod would arrive home in a state of abject misery and I didn't know how to help my husband, or my son.

One Sunday evening when he returned from Churinga, Rod surprised me with a confident smile. "Next Sunday I'll let Dane steer the car up Churinga's drive. That will give him something good to focus on."

Rod's simple logic amazed and delighted me. Churinga's long straight driveway ran from the front entrance to a rear car park. This was ideal for a teen learning to drive and I shared Rod's confidence that steering the car would give Dane something to look forward to on those bleak Sunday nights.

Rod and I discussed this plan from every angle. We decided to change the way we spoke to Dane about returning to Churinga on Sunday nights. We abandoned expressions such as "It's time to go back to Churinga" for the more positive "Your friends will be waiting for you at Churinga." Then I'd add, "And Dad's going to let you steer the car!"

Rod's plan worked wonders. Dane couldn't wait to bound indoors and tell everyone at Churinga that he'd driven the car. In no time he was looking forward to Sunday nights. "My Dad lets me drive the car. I'm an excellent driver!" he'd tell anyone who would listen, just like the Dustin Hoffman character in the wonderful movie *Rain Man.*

As a child, Dane's love of trees had expanded into an interest in other countries. His favorite book, *The Red Balloon*, where all those lovely balloons flew off to Pascal in Paris, reinforced this interest. He began to ask questions like: Where is Paris? Where is France? Rod bought a map of the world and after years of patient explanations Dane eventually grasped the concept of countries and oceans, and of why it took so long to travel from place to place.

After Dane had settled into Churinga, his godmother, Margaret, put an exciting proposition to me. "We know Dane loves lakes and rivers. Why don't you and Dane come home with me to Fiji for a vacation?"

At this stage, Dane was struggling through the most traumatic years of his life. I badly needed a vacation but, looking back, I wonder how on earth we found the courage to contemplate this excursion.

The volume of paperwork relating to Dane's reservation was overwhelming. The venture would only succeed if Dane had a window seat to watch the clouds and if he could disembark the moment the plane doors opened as he was very intolerant of lines. We knew this was the only way to avoid tantrums. But I ran foul of the airline's computer! The computer obeyed company policy to the letter, insisting that anyone with a disability must sit next to the aisle and disembark at the end of the line.

This was just what we didn't want for Dane. I spent hours repeating my requests and explanations. A different person answered the phone each time I called the airline. Time after time I'd launch into lengthy explanations but negotiation was impossible. No one dared argue with the computer.

I was just about to consider trying another airline, when Margaret suggested we contact the Qantas Customer Sales Consultant, a woman who arranged travel for the Cluny sisters to and from the world's most isolated and impoverished countries. She could overrule the computer. And she did!

With a window seat and the opportunity to watch clouds I believed Dane would last the distance. I just hoped there wouldn't be too many crying babies on board. Rod and I role-played to prepare Dane for the flight. I'd act the role of the flight attendant asking, "Would you like tea or coffee, sir?" I'd demonstrate how the attendant would serve lunch and dinner and how the tray would fold down from behind the seat in front of him. We explained how passengers would be having conversations, and that babies might be crying, and why there might be delays at customs.

Our five-hour flight to Nandi was incident free. The airline staff were very helpful, Dane loved the clouds and enjoyed the on-board activity, and we were the first to disembark. And from the moment we arrived I felt as though I belonged in Fiji. Margaret's warm, compassionate family made us very welcome. We visited her friends, ate and sang, swam in the lagoons and walked along the beaches. Dane was so calm that Margaret suggested we venture farther afield to visit her extended family on Matagi Island. This meant a flight to Taveuni Island and then a boat trip to Matagi.

A nasty storm closed Suva's Nausori Airport on the day we were to make this journey. We left the following day in a small plane without a co-pilot or a flight attendant. I read the emergency procedures, just in case. Life jackets are stored under the seat I read. I felt under my seat but couldn't locate a life jacket. I caught the eye of another passenger who shrugged and shook his head. I could see where the fire extinguisher should have been, close to the pilot's seat. It wasn't there. The pilot was using it! He was directing a stream of foam underneath the control panel and within minutes thick smoke billowed from the cockpit. Margaret nervously recited her rosary while Dane gazed at the clouds oblivious to the drama.

I felt numb with disbelief. It was as though we were trapped in a terrifying dream. I took a waterproof felt-tip pen from my bag and wrote notes to Rod on the inside of my forearm. I'd hug this arm tightly against my chest as the plane went down. I had to let him know how much I loved him.

Eventually the plane began its descent. Through the choking smoke in the cabin I could see land, and an airport! Now Dane became very concerned and asked, "What's the pilot landing here for? We're back at Suva!"

"Are we, Dane? Are you sure this is Suva?"

"Yes, Mum. That's the Nausori River down there, and there's the Nausori airport!"

Trust Dane to recognize the landscape. We landed safely and I forgot the messages on my arm until curious stares reminded me!

Storms closed Nausori Airport again the following day but eventually we took off in another aircraft. Thankfully it didn't ignite and we landed at Taveuni in teeming rain. An open-topped vehicle waited near a taxi sign. "Excuse me, is this a taxi?" "Yes, this is the taxi!" "Can you take us to the boat for Matagi Island?" Yes, the driver would be pleased to take us to the boat.

As he tucked our luggage under a tarpaulin, Margaret donned a plastic poncho. She knew what to expect: no shelter was provided. Dane was highly amused—fancy sitting in the rain on purpose!

Our taxi left the little township and turned into a narrow dirt road. We splashed and bounced under a dense canopy of overhanging trees and vines and stopped in a small waterfront clearing. The driver opened the doors, took our luggage out from under the tarpaulin, put it on the ground and announced, "Man with the boat will come!" Then he jumped behind the wheel and disappeared back into that towering, dripping jungle.

We peered through the rain. There was definitely no boat. Nor was there a wharf, a jetty, or even a pontoon. Just us and a beach and all those trees. How would the man in the boat know where we were? Or even that we were anywhere?

We began to laugh. Margaret was as wet inside her poncho as she was on the outside. She looked at me and spluttered, "Junee, your hair—you look like a wet mop!"

Dane began to laugh too. He'd never seen his mother and his godmother in such a state! For once I envied Dane his casual clothes. I'd bought a pretty floral dress with a softly gathered, calf-length skirt. I'd pictured myself walking barefoot along white sandy beaches, skirt wafting gently in the tropical breezes. Now it slapped around my legs and clung like wet plastic-wrap. Stiletto-heeled sandals were another poor choice for a wet day in the jungle.

We stood in the rain laughing at each other until we became mildly hysterical. Then a shout from the jungle startled us. A man appeared through the trees and asked, "Are you going to Matagi Island?" "Yes, we are!" "You come with me." We hesitated and he disappeared back into the trees. He reappeared and called again, "You come with me to the boat!"

We picked up our luggage and plunged into the dense jungle. My stiletto heels sank into the mud on the narrow path and as I tried to gather my wet skirt between my legs like a giant diaper I wished I'd brought a big safety pin. We struggled onto another beach where a small open boat bobbed in shallow water. We followed our boatman into the water, scrambled aboard and headed off to sea in the rain. Each time we'd catch one another's eye, we'd collapse into another fit of laughter.

As we neared Matagi Island I could see Margaret's friends and relatives on the beach, smiling and waving flowers and playing musical instruments. They appeared oblivious to the rain. Grasping the dead weight of my wet skirt between my legs, I half fell out of the boat at their feet. So much for creating a good impression.

Matagi Island was as magnificent as our traditional welcome. We were surrounded by rugged mountaintops covered with jungle and by coral reefs said to be among the most spectacular on the planet. The sun broke through and I'd never seen water sparkle as it did around this island. We walked along beaches with sand like talcum powder, never seeing another human footprint.

The lush tropical climate, the different culture and the native Fijians' dark, lustrous skin intrigued Dane. "How can I have skin like that, Mum?" he asked me. I tried to explain how this depends on one's parents and I'm certain he felt Rod and I had failed him. He enjoyed the traditional music and ate second helpings of the unfamiliar food. This young man who so intensely disliked change embraced all these differences with enthusiasm.

Fiji was a nourishing and strengthening experience for us all. We shared much joy with Margaret and her warm and loving extended family. Happy faces in our vacation photographs remind us of the laughter and fun we experienced there, and of a subtle shift in Dane's attitude. He began to relax a little, no longer stiffening if I asked him for a hug, or flinching if I touched him.

When we returned home, the Cluny sisters honored Dane's sixteenth birthday with a celebratory Mass. He understood how unique and special this was. He was almost bursting with joy when, after Mass, he rode in a horse-drawn carriage to the city where we all met for *yum cha*, his friend Erin by his side. Later one of the sisters, Sister Valerie, recalled her lasting image of Dane's sheer delight in just being alive. She said he challenged those places within herself that did not know how to live life to the fullest.

Dane's enjoyment of his birthday and of our visit to Fiji was miraculous—he'd demonstrated so little emotion before his teens. Yet happy interludes such as these were usually followed by inexplicable, ever-deepening, black depressions.

Nice of you to teach me

Dane was lying on the ground in our backyard, eyes closed and very still. I watched him for a while, then I felt I had to speak to him.

"Excuse me, Dane," I said quietly, "but you've been here for *so* long. What are you doing?"

He replied, "I'm waiting to die."

The words cut through my soul like a razor. I'd learned to withdraw from pain but this was unbearable. However, I knew I couldn't let Dane see my distress. I had to stay calm so he could draw on that calmness.

"Do you really feel so sad and so lost? Is there anything I can do?"

"No, Mum."

"Well, Dane, please remember that I love you."

That was all I could do. Go back to the love.

Not long after this, I found Dane staring for a long, long time at water running from a tap, holding his hand in the flow. I kept my distance, hoping the running water might calm him. Then I asked tentatively, "Dane, aren't your hands clean now? Perhaps you'd like a bucket of water?"

"No. I'm waiting to drown myself."

Within an hour of both these incidents Dane was behaving as though nothing amiss had taken place.

As Dane's depressions intensified, we realized he needed extra help. As a psychologist, Vicki Bitsika wasn't qualified to prescribe medication, and as Dr. John was in Sydney, I didn't know where to turn. We'd wasted so much time and money with the "doll's house" psychiatrist.

Then a dreadful incident occurred on our way to an appointment with Vicki Bitsika. Here is what happened in Vicki's words:

I heard a terrible screech of brakes right outside the house. I didn't take much notice until someone knocked on the front door and I opened it and saw Junee's face. I half carried her into the house as Dane shuffled about, obviously very agitated.

I said, "You wait in our room, Dane. I need to talk to your mum."

As I closed the door behind us Junee just looked at me. She was trembling in every limb. She whispered, "Vicki, he tried to kill himself. He stepped in front of a truck."

This wasn't about a childhood fascination for moving wheels. Dane knew exactly what he wanted to do and he'd figured out how to do it. He had deliberately stepped off the curb into the path of the truck. The traffic was moving quickly, but somehow the driver had managed to stop in time.

What were we to do? Then, in answer to our prayers, Dr. John returned to Melbourne. After long consultations and a period of keeping records, he diagnosed rapid cycle mood swings. He changed Dane's medication and within a few days the mood swings began to diminish. What a relief that was.

I raised the subject of Dane's sexuality with Dr. John. With Vicki's encouragement, we'd given Dane an illustrated publication dealing with teenage sexuality, but I was concerned that, as with everything else, we might need to explain matters in more detail. Also could his problems be influenced by sexual repression? Dr. John didn't think so. He suggested we do no more. To introduce topics he wasn't ready for would only add to Dane's confusion. He would make us aware if and when he needed more information.

With correct medication and Vicki Bitsika's on-going counseling, Dane's life (and ours) improved markedly. He began part-time work in a coffee shop and in the kitchen at La Verna, and in the kitchen at the Austin Hospital. Given clear and simple instructions about specific tasks, he was a willing worker and appeared to relate well to people prepared to help him.

I joined Churinga's Committee of Management, accepting this responsibility primarily out of gratitude for the help Dane was receiving, but also because it gave me a sense of self-worth. I knew I could contribute, and I also knew that organizations like Churinga relied on the parents to help maintain and develop services for children with special needs.

When rumors started to appear that Churinga was to close, the committee gave little credence to them. Recent changes in government policy required schools with boarding facilities to eventually relocate the residential component into the larger community. Alternatively, the educational component could relocate. The government didn't want beds and desks under the same roof, so to speak. But as a committee we weren't unduly concerned. Churinga had received an excellent government assessment in the lead-up to these new policies. There was never any suggestion that this boarding school should close.

Then Churinga's government funding was reduced. This may have been a subtle incentive to initiate the required changes but at no time were we told to make haste. Even if pressure had been placed on us, we knew we had ample funds to stay open until every student had been properly relocated. Finding new schools and accommodations for all these youngsters—each with his or her own special needs—would be a huge undertaking

Within days of the funding cut, the St. John of God Brothers issued written advice that Churinga would close its doors in four weeks. They cited the combination of funding cuts and changed government policy as an attempt to justify their decision. Despite our pleas, they could not be dissuaded. Just go away now, thank you. We're closing the doors.

Through its new policy, the government was dismantling one structure without building another, and now the Churinga parents faced the seemingly impossible task of finding properly supervised accommodations and appropriate schooling within reasonable commuting distance. Added to this was the looming prospect of the long summer vacations. The Churinga parents were emotionally and financially shattered. In one tragic instance a young parent attempted to end her life.

Parents and staff joined forces and fought desperately to postpone the Brothers' decision. I was appointed the spokesperson for this group. One evening when Rod arrived home from work I was still in my dressing gown; the phone hadn't stopped ringing all day. When I got up the next morning, I broke down and cried. I remember Rod saying, "All you have to do today is shower and dress because you might need to answer the door, too!" I think I smiled for the first time in days.

Media support for the Churinga parents was outstanding. Dane and I appeared on ABC TV and the host's incisive questions helped me to state our case for postponing Churinga's closure. I also had a meeting with the Community Services Minister, Caroline Hogg. She made it perfectly clear that she also supported a postponement. Then the Minister and her staff met with the Brothers, but despite the pleas, and another flurry of media attention, the Brothers would not reconsider. They would not postpone Churinga's closure.

After the school had closed, an officer from Community Services Victoria phoned me at home to recommend a facility for Dane. This was another combined educational–residential facility, so while it may also have been under the shadow of closure at least this was something. It had an immediate vacancy and it was in a country town; Dane always preferred to be in the country.

Rod and I were very hopeful and made an appointment to visit the facility on the weekend. A few days later Rod phoned from work. He was obviously very upset.

"Have you heard the news?" he asked. When I asked what news, he said, "I think you should buy a newspaper. And forget about Saturday."

I ran to our neighborhood store and bought a paper. There on the front page was the devastating story of the deaths of a number of young people at the very same facility we had planned to visit. Fifty-one assault charges were to be made. Surely the officer from Community Services who had suggested this placement must have known about this. Surely we deserved a warning.

By early the following year Community Services had located placements for most Churinga students. Dane, however, was one of a small group for whom this was proving extremely difficult. After protracted negotiations with the St. John of God Brothers, it was resolved that Churinga's residential section would temporarily reopen to accommodate these students and that they would attend the nearby Concord School until the end of June. Despite the excellent staff at the Concord School, we only just survived those six months, but at least it gave us breathing space.

In this troubled chain of events, one link shone like gold. Dane was able to continue seeing the speech therapist from Churinga, Margaret Uren. When addressing another person, Dane spoke in a stilted, statement-like manner and he had difficulty maintaining a conversation. He repeated or re-phrased other people's comments without offering his own thoughts or opinions. Alone, he mumbled and thought aloud in the characteristic way of people with autism.

Margaret Uren employed a variety of techniques to modify Dane's loud voice but she did it in such a way that he didn't see these as lessons. She would talk about the things that were important to him. She would introduce new words and concepts. They might discuss vacations, or artists, or a poet. Dane began to enjoy rhyming words so she introduced poetry about trees and the wind, the moon and the sea. Margaret Uren dealt with the whole person, not just that person's disability or speech problems.

Like Vicki Bitsika, she urged Dane to use his diary, en-couraging him to record his observations, ideas and feelings. In this way she expanded his communication skills. One entry in his diary was pure poetry: "I dream wild wind. I dreamed the stars in the sky all came tumbling down. They covered all of the town, road and hill."

As a mother, Margaret Uren understood the wrench we felt sending Dane off to school every Sunday, and she under-stood that for us this diary provided a link between school and home. I am sure we learned more from reading Dane's diary each weekend than if we'd sat beside him each and every day.

She also used the diary as source material. She would expand Dane's news into an exercise. Using Dane's news, Dane's words, made the exercise relevant to him: "We had lunch in Beechworth. I saw autumn leaves. They are very beautiful. Leaves change. CHANGE, RANGE, ARRANGE! The trees are very shady and green and lovely in summer. We need the shade to keep the hot off us. At Yarrawonga we picked pumpkins. I like pumpkin."

Dane's speech improved markedly under Margaret Uren's tutelage, but she was more than just a speech therapist. She was also a remarkable teacher of life skills. She helped Dane cope with puberty and take control of his own life, and she encouraged him to consider the effect of his attitudes on those around him. He became aware of other people's opinions. *Oh, you have thoughts, too! You have ideas that interest me!*

It wasn't until he began to emerge from his dreadful adolescent depressions that Dane *needed* to communicate. All that hard work by skilled teachers during his childhood was an excellent preparation for this. Now, at around sixteen and a half, he was ready to write a few words or a sentence and he began reading for the sheer pleasure of recognizing and discovering the words! He'd read a short, simple magazine article about something that interested him. And he could read and remember signs, directions and instructions.

Dane worked with Margaret Uren for four years. In their last session together she asked him what he would remember of their lessons. She expected him to say, "Speak well."

He smiled at her and paused to consider his answer.

"Speak softly, speak normally." Then he added, "Nice of you to teach me!"

Dane discovered his own "natural therapy," too. He did this with the Colegrave family at Stringybark Farm in the mountains near Healesville. I had made friends with Vicki Colegrave at Warrawong. Being truly gifted with young people with special needs she was totally at ease with Dane. From the moment we arrived for our first visit to Stringybark Farm he was more settled than he'd been for months. As we were leaving, Vicki and her husband Michael invited Dane to be their guest from time to time. We could see they were serious. Dane had enjoyed helping Michael on the farm and they saw an opportunity for him to relate to their own three children in a family situation.

These visits became a monthly routine and brought much joy in those difficult years. With the three Colegrave children, Toby, Tom and Annie, Dane would swim, "ride" a surfboard and row a boat on the farm dam. They would cut and stack hay and collect firewood for the big slow-combustion heater. After lunch one day Vicki was stretched out in an armchair watching Dane stack kindling beside the barbecue when she briefly dozed off. When she woke up, the substantial brick barbecue had completely disappeared under a mountain of sticks!

Michael's praise for Dane when he cut the grass around the house and through the kiwifruit vines gave him a wonderful sense of achievement. One day when Dane was mowing they heard a clattering noise, as though twigs were catching in the blades. Dane had finished the house yard and was mowing the adjoining forest!

He felt very involved in the work and in the fun. If something needed doing he'd say, "They should clean that up, shouldn't they Vicki?" This was his way of asking her permission to do the job himself. This interaction with the Colegrave family really empowered Dane as he struggled with his own self-worth. He knew they really wanted him to visit. Proudly he'd say, "And when I get to Vicki's farm, I can help!"

The house at Stringybark Farm was a two-story building with a spacious veranda overlooking glorious mountain views. Each night after dinner Vicki and Michael would encourage Dane to spend his quiet time alone here, watching the sunset reflecting in the dam. Late one evening Michael let Dane join him on the hayshed roof while he screwed down new cladding under portable lights. Dane sat quietly in the center of the roof. Suddenly Michael realized he'd disappeared. Quickly he climbed down to look for him. He searched the surrounding area, then the creek and the dam but there was sign of Dane. Frantically Michael rushed back to the house where he found Dane alone on the veranda watching a rising moon.

Dane loved to stand on the veranda as summer lightning skipped from mountain to mountain. On one spectacular evening Toby Colegrave joined him and with each flash they'd call to Vicki, "Did you see that one!" Vicki sensed they were daring each other to confront the storm. She was about to warn them to come inside when a nearby tree erupted into a shower of sparks and a crash of thunder shook the house. Vicki was convinced Dane's feet didn't touch the floor as he and Toby flew indoors! Later they found their telephone melted to the wall.

Vicki and Michael knew Dane could control his explosive anger if necessary. They understood the importance of consistency and maintained Vicki Bitsika's programs. Quietly they'd say "No, I don't think so, Dane" at any sign of inappropriate behavior. Vicki cannot remember any time when Dane became angry or distressed. Only once, when the children were having a rare argument, did he appear uncomfortable. He couldn't understand the change in the children's demeanor.

Dane learned so much from Toby, Tom and Annie. They expected nothing and imposed no conditions on him. He adopted their expressions and behavior and body language. When the time approached for him to leave, they'd count the weeks before he'd be back on a calendar saying, "We'll look forward to seeing you on this date, Dane, in exactly four weeks!" The visual clues made it bearable for him to say goodbye.

Dane had never wavered in his resolve to move into a mobile home beside the Murray River. We floundered with this until, after lengthy negotiations, Dane bought a friend's old van with his earnings from his work placements. At the invitation of the Cluny sisters we placed the van discreetly on the grounds of Cluny Convent. Of course, this was a compromise and, whereas one reason would have satisfied anyone else, Dane required on-going explanations as to why he couldn't park his van beside the Murray River. Despite this he loved Cluny, and he was proud to have his own "home" where he could invite his special friend Erin or Rod's parents to afternoon tea.

This was Dane's first experience with independence. With the support of his godmother he could stay in his own van if and when he wished, on weekends and during school vacations. The van remained at Cluny for several years.

Dane was now overcoming the worst of his depressions, and he was anxious to move back home from Churinga and find a job. Before applying for regular employment, he needed to undergo the preparatory training available at certain special schools linked to selected TAFE (Technical and Further Education) colleges that provided Work Education courses. There was no such school within reasonable distance of Brunswick, so the logical thing to do was to find Dane suitable accommodations near one of these schools.

Logic, though, didn't apply in this situation. The guidelines clearly stated that Dane could not live in a government-funded group home outside his own residential area. I was juggling with a bureaucracy gone mad. After months of beating on doors, including yet again that of Community Services Minister, I finally managed to have this regulation set aside. Of course, there was a catch. Dane's residential funding could only be used outside Brunswick if he shared his accommodation with other Churinga students.

So began our search for a group home near a suitable school. After hearing "Sorry, no vacancies" time and time again, we realized we would have to establish our own group home. Again I did the rounds of officialdom, learning that if parents of ex-Churinga students jointly rented, furnished and provisioned a suitable house, the government would fund staff to supervise the boys.

So now I had to identify an appropriate special school linked to a TAFE college, locate a suitable rental house, and find at least four ex-Churinga students with whom Dane could share. Eventually we found a special school in Dandenong, thirty-five kilometers from Brunswick, which was linked to the TAFE college there. I located four students of similar age and needs as Dane, and after long discussions with the young men and their parents, and with the consent of all concerned, including Dane, we rented a house in Dandenong and Dane began his course.

The government-employed carers were enthusiastic and energetic and did their utmost for these five individual and quite demanding young men. They worked hard to maintain harmony and keep the boy's behavior within reasonable limits, and they dealt with difficult situations skillfully and tactfully. They celebrated birthdays and anniversaries and took every opportunity to have fun.

We expected Dane would choose to spend occasional weekends at the home in Dandenong, but instead he asked me to pick him up promptly after classes every Friday afternoon. It was vital to be on time or he'd become upset. And he was never eager to return on Sunday nights. Despite a big welcome from the other lads, he always looked forlorn. Rod's heart almost broke every week as Dane sorrowfully waved him farewell. He would agonize over whether we had made the right decision.

Rod faced those dismal Sunday nights for one and a half years, but we couldn't back down. Dane had to learn to function in a workplace situation and this wouldn't be possible if he lived at home.

Dane was very proud when Erin Young asked him to be her partner at a debutante ball organized by Bulleen Special School where Erin was still a student. This remarkable event generated enormous excitement and Dane and Erin were very excited to be a part of it. For months before he went to Dandenong, I happily drove Dane across Melbourne—from Churinga to Bulleen—for practice sessions.

Finally the big night arrived. Dane and Erin were driven to the ball in a limousine. Erin looked beautiful in her beautiful gown. "Oh, Junee," she said, "it's just like a wedding, isn't it?" A skilled and patient dressmaker had made this gown for Erin, ensuring the unfinished garment was ready to try on the moment Erin arrived for each fitting.

Dane's face lit up with delight when we entered the beautifully decorated ballroom. Then he gasped, "Oh, Mum, look at that!"

It wasn't the exquisite table decorations that attracted his attention. It was the balloons. Clouds of orange and white balloons floated above the dance floor and filled every corner of the room. Orange balloons! They could have been chosen just for Dane! Was it really only ten years since he feared opening a Christmas package to find his own orange balloon?

I was so proud when Dane asked me to dance. Once he has learned a sequence of events he'll remember them exactly, and this applied equally well to his new dancing skills. Confidently he led me onto the floor. My feet hardly touched the ground as I glided around on my son's arm.

Erin's debut was a highlight for Dane in the midst of a difficult time in his life. He glowed with pleasure that wonderful evening. The official photographer dubbed him "Mister Opal Smile"!

A remarkable life

Despite his sadness at leaving us on Sunday nights, Dane settled into a routine at his group home. He responded positively to on-going counseling with Vicki Bitsika and his monthly visits to the Colegrave family at Stringybark Farm helped to counter the effects of the noise and bustle of Dandenong, and the pressures of TAFE and work placements. Plus he was achieving his objective. By the summer of 1992, he had a three-hours-per-week work placement in the assembly plant at Rosebank Industries and he worked as a kitchen hand for one day a week at McDonald's. Later that year he worked at Mitre 10 and Telstra.

Although these work placements meant a great deal to Dane, and could have led to longer-term work in the area when he completed his course, he was adamant that he wanted to come home to live with us when he finished college at the end of the year. However, commuting from Brunswick to Dandenong was out of the question for Dane and we couldn't move there; it would have been much too far for Rod to travel to work.

So where would we all live when Dane finished his course? Bearing in mind his love of the country, we investigated rural Victoria for work opportunities but the prospects were dim. By now I could have written "The Melbourne Guidebook to Work Placements and Accommodation for People with Special Needs," and it looked to me as if Dandenong might be Dane's only option. This question weighed very heavily on our minds.

Another thing which worried us dreadfully at this time was Rod's health. For some time now he had been suffering badly from ulcers but had chosen to ignore his doctor's warnings about overwork. When he went for his next three-monthly gastroscopy, the doctor bluntly informed him that if he didn't change his lifestyle drastically, he'd be dead before his next appointment.

I'd been unwell too. After I visited various specialists for different symptoms, a neurologist suggested the possibility of multiple sclerosis. He arranged for me to have a magnetic resonance imaging scan but with only one scanning unit in Melbourne I faced a harrowing three-month wait. (This was eventually diagnosed as an arthritic condition. All those years of tense, long drives around Melbourne had damaged my neck and shoulder.)

As Dane was on vacation with Margaret Whitcombe at this time, Rod suggested he and I ride the Harley to Sydney to try to forget about our health problems and to see what Sydney had to offer in the way of work for Dane and housing for us all.

So, with letters of introduction to the New South Wales Autistic Centre tucked into the saddlebag, we donned helmets and leathers and headed north on the Black Wizard. It's amazing how those heavy black clothes disguise advancing years! We felt like a pair of escaping teenagers. And we felt optimistic that we'd find our solutions in Sydney. Rod already operated a large client base there and we knew his company would arrange a transfer from Melbourne.

Sydney's educational facilities for young people with special needs were impressive, but our hopes were crushed.

There was no likelihood of work for Dane anywhere near where we would want to live or near Rod's work. We checked every possibility, but found there was nothing to be gained by relocating.

This was bitterly disappointing but at least Rod and I were together on the Harley in the midst of a glorious summer. Perhaps forest roads and ocean views would lift our spirits. We decided to return home via the coast road.

Our first port of call was Campbelltown where we visited the Poor Clare nuns, a contemplative order I'd made contact with through La Verna. Rod was concerned about the nuns' reaction to our arrival—"We can't ride the Harley into a monastery!"—but they were very pleased to see us. And they were very impressed with the Harley-Davidson, too; that they knew how special these bikes were amazed Rod.

We talked openly with these good people and asked for their prayers. Sister Clare placed me on her prayer list, suggested books for me to read, and invited me to retreat with her community. I have since done this and we've all remained good friends. I've often asked for their special prayers during Dane's most difficult crises.

The NSW Autistic Centre had suggested a number of facilities on the NSW south coast. We checked each of these but there was nothing for Dane. A black depression settled on us. Our problems seemed overwhelming. We rode down the coast through Nowra and Bateman's Bay and paused for lunch at Narooma, scarcely noticing the beautiful countryside. Rod asked if we should phone Llewyn and Greer at Bega. I burst into tears. I didn't want our friends to see us in this state.

As we rode through lovely Cobargo, Rod suddenly swung the bike off the Princes Highway onto a side road. "Let's stay at Bermagui!" he called over his shoulder to me. As we traveled through spotted-gum forests to this popular seaside resort, I wondered how on earth we'd find an accommodation there in mid-summer, but I said nothing.

Rod parked the bike on the main street outside a motel. It had stunning views of the coastline and towering Mount Dromedary. To our astonishment there was a vacancy, and the motel owner offered us a room with a balcony overlooking that view!

Noticing our helmets and leather jackets, she asked about the bike. A Harley, indeed! Rod asked if we could park it undercover.

With a conspiratorial look at me she said, "I know what these men are like about their Harleys, dear."

Then she said to Rod, "Would you like to park it in the hall outside your unit? It won't be in the way."

Aghast, I interrupted, "Surely not on the carpet!"

"Oh yes, on the carpet."

Then, with a knowing look at Rod, she said, "Harleys don't drip oil, do they?"

"Oh, no," he stammered. "Harleys don't drip oil. Indeed not!"

So while Rod and I slept to the sound of the ocean, the Black Wizard waited outside our door. I just hoped it wouldn't disgrace itself on the hall carpet.

The following morning we awoke refreshed and revived. The cheerful kindness of the motel owner had eased our depression. I'm certain the prayers of the Poor Clare nuns guided us to this remarkable woman's motel.

After a leisurely breakfast, we watched fishing trawlers unloading the morning's catch. We bought take-out cappuccino and sat in a lovely park, admiring the water and the distant mountain.

Immediately we finished our coffee, Rod asked, "What will we do now?"

We laughed. This was what Dane would have said, and for once Rod and I were free to do absolutely nothing!

We had checked into the motel for one night, but we stayed for three. We walked along the beaches, ate fish and chips, and sipped wine on our balcony. As we relaxed we began to feel more positive.

"How about we do phone Greer and Llewyn?" Rod suggested.

I agreed, so Rod rang and asked if we could come and say hello. They insisted we stay at least one night.

We hadn't intended to unload our problems on Greer and Llewyn but everything just tumbled out. Llewyn suggested we see what Bega had to offer. As he spoke I remembered something Pat Leevers had said way back in 1979 after we'd read *Autistic Children*. She'd mentioned Bega's excellent facilities for people with intellectual disabilities.

We met the manager of Bega's Tulgeen, a residential, educational and employment support service for adults with intellectual disabilities. We were very impressed with Tulgeen's Riverside Plant Nursery, its Work Crew, who carry out repairs and maintenance and gardening jobs, and Stitches and Prints, a calico tote-bag manufacturing business run by the service.

Here was a country town offering facilities we couldn't find in Melbourne or Sydney. At long last we dared to be hopeful. I thanked God for that warm welcome at Bermagui.

We arranged for Dane to visit Llewyn and Greer so we could gauge his reaction to Bega and its facilities. He spent time at Tulgeen where he experienced an immediate rapport. He could see for himself that we could live at Bega as a family unit and that he could find employment there. The winds of change felt so refreshing.

As a family we had always enjoyed celebrating special occasions and the following Mother's Day was no exception. After taking me to lunch Rod and Dane announced that we were to take a short drive into the country where I would receive my gift. In a paddock near Olinda, high in the Dandenong Ranges, I was presented with a heifer calf. She was a purebred Dexter, and her name was Azure. I was speechless!

Dane knew exactly what Rod had in mind. He said, "Well, we've got the cow. Now we'll have to get a farm!"

At that moment I knew Rod would retire from work and we'd move to Bega. We'd done our arithmetic and discussed the prospect at length. If we had a farm in the Bega Valley we'd be a full-time family again. We really wanted to do this. Little Azure settled the matter. She was Rod's way of saying, *We've made up our minds. Let's go!*

We needed a prefix to register Azure with the Dexter breed society, and to identify the purebred Dexter beef cattle stud we planned to breed. We decided to use the first two letters in each of our names. The little black calf would be known as Da'Juro Azure.

On the evening of Dane's eighteenth birthday we toasted our son and our future as a family. On that same day we'd signed a contract for land in the Bega Valley, and we chose the name of the home we would build there: it too would be known as Da'Juro.

Two days later we drove to Bega for a weekend with Llewyn and Greer, soon to be our next-door neighbors. The next morning we fell into earnest discussion about the new house. As Rod and Llewyn deliberated over levels and falls, I could feel myself sliding into overload. Heavens, we'd only signed up for the land three days before! Greer quietly left the room and reappeared with a picnic basket, cushions and a blanket. In the basket lay a chilled bottle of wine, chilled glasses and pre-lunch nibbles.

She said, "Look, you two. Just sit on the rock and relax, and enjoy a drink together! We'll join you later with Dane."

The rock to which Greer referred was an outcropping of smooth stone commanding a superb view of the valley— a view we hoped to frame in the windows of our new home. We'll never forget that magical morning, sipping wine on "our" rock in glorious winter sunshine. Out of this interlude came decisions we have been content to live with.

Dane faced a major disappointment when chickenpox prevented him from attending a christening in the Bega Valley. He had been delighted when Rod and I were invited to become the godparents of Ray Ryan's baby son, Nicholas. We had met Ray and Cheryl at a barbecue at Bega and had subsequently engaged Ray to build our new house. When we told Dane he could only come with us to Bega if he was prepared to remain in isolation at Llewyn and Greer's home, he agreed. For the first time in his life, he dealt positively with a disappointment.

Dane's emerging maturity was displayed again when he went to a wedding on his own. Dane was invited as a friend of the bride who was one of the carers at the group home in Dandenong. This was his first such experience without us and by all accounts he enjoyed himself immensely. He was growing up.

It was around this time that Dane also had to deal with the death of Jaeger. This active, intelligent companion had lived all her life behind high fences, and we were looking forward to taking her to Bega's wonderful open spaces. But it was not to be. One Saturday night I was awakened by her scratching at the back door. Her abdomen was terribly swollen. Our vet was away for the weekend so I rushed her to an emergency clinic. Dane and I sat with her the next day, but I could see she wasn't improving as we held her and stroked her as best we could through all sorts of tests.

On the Monday morning we transferred her to our local vet. He began exploratory surgery but it was too late. Did we want to say goodbye?

When our beautiful friend lay on the operating table, beyond pain, I burst into tears.

"Her spirit will go up to heaven, won't it, Mum?" Dane asked. I agreed without hesitation. I didn't feel a bit sacrilegious. How could this loyal creature be overlooked in the grand scheme of things?

Later Dane asked, "When are we going to have Jaeger's funeral?" Without thinking I said, "Oh, Dane, that's too difficult for us. The vet will have a funeral for Jaeger." I could see he was bitterly disappointed. "But Mum, we didn't give her flowers! And we didn't say any prayers!"

I suggested we buy flowers at the nearby Victoria Markets. We walked home in silence and Dane reverently placed the flowers inside Jaeger's empty kennel. We sat quietly and he said a prayer for his friend. He was comfortable with this tangible farewell. I felt better too. On this occasion Dane helped me to cope.

Dane missed Jaeger terribly. "Do you miss Jaeger, Mum?" he'd say.

"Yes, Dane, I miss Jaeger very much."

I had to give him "permission" to be sad, and reassure him that sorrow was a natural reaction to the loss of a friend.

Jaeger was nine years old when she died. They'd been together for half Dane's lifetime.

Jaeger's death marked the final chapter of our life in Brunswick. We placed our house on the market, and began our farewells. Breaking our ties with Melbourne wasn't easy, especially for Rod. He was at the height of his career, and he enjoyed the challenge of his work, the travel and the entertaining. He had many farewells, and they were all very special.

I had many wonderful farewells too. The most memorable was held on a glorious day in the gardens of the Warrawong Day Care Kindergarten. On our eighteen-year journey with autism we'd crossed the paths of so many loving, supportive people. Now, seemingly, they were all here to wish us well.

As we mingled with our friends, each smile echoed the highs and lows of our journey. Each smile confirmed that we had made the right choices. Especially Dane's smile! Dane, the little boy who'd arrived at this kindergarten without speech or any need for love or friendship or human contact, was laughing and talking. The little boy who wouldn't be touched was hugging his devoted godmother, Margaret, and my friend Toni, without whom I might not have survived his first year. The little boy who'd screamed if others came close was mingling with all sorts of people: with Pat Leevers who changed our lives with a book, with Kath and Geoff Nicholls who minded him so I could go to Hong Kong, with Joan Groube for whom he sang "Happy Birthday" before he could speak, with Liz Gower who helped us to understand echolalia.

He was happy and proud to welcome Kiely-Lynn Waters, his "sister," Vicki Bitsika, without whom we might not have survived his early teens, and his friend Erin Young and her parents, with whom he had shared many vacations. He offered sandwiches to officials I'd consulted with over funding issues, to our local member of Parliament, and to current and former staff members of Warrawong and Irabina, including his former teachers.

I experienced the joys and the sorrow of parting as I watched Dane with all the parents associated with the Warrawong Family Support Group. With the encouragement of Warrawong's Director and my friend Liz Gower, I'd helped to establish this group and for five years we shared information and activities and gave ourselves permission to be optimistic and positive, and to laugh!

I was humbled to receive a testimonial that day, but I was proud to accept it with Rod and Dane by my side. It said:

Presented to Junee Waites in recognition and
appreciation of her outstanding contribution to
families of children with disabilities as a compassionate
support person, advisor and friend and as a tenacious
campaigner for the rights of these children. From
the Mayor and Councillors, City of Ringwood, 12
December 1992.

Before we left Melbourne, we had one final consultation with Dr. John. As we took our leave, he took Dane's hand and shook it vigorously, saying, "Dane! I don't have any doubts!"

Then he continued slowly and deliberately, "You . . . are going to have . . . a remarkable life!"

My heart sank momentarily. A remarkable life? Couldn't Dr. John have suggested a quiet life? What if Bega proved to be less than remarkable? We could be in big trouble.

Dane smiled confidently as he shook his doctor's hand and replied, "Yes, I know. A remarkable life!"

The running singlet

A flautist's haunting melody ushered evening into night. Dane sat spellbound, then he looked up and smiled as a breeze rustled overhanging leaves. Rod gave me a knowing nudge. Leaves! Our son still marveled at the movement of leaves.

We were gathered beside the dam at Stringybark Farm where Dane had spent so many wonderful weekends. We sang Christmas carols and shared friendships and picnic baskets. The following day we would begin our new life in peaceful farmland, between the mountains and the sea.

Hundreds of candles reflected in the still, dark water. Those glowing candles spoke so clearly of choices and hope, and of love. I thanked God for our joys while I fed the pain and chaos of Dane's first eighteen years into those cleansing flames. I had no need for excess baggage.

The next day we left Melbourne for our new home in Bega. We had arranged for the movers to collect our belongings and take them as far as Merimbula, just south of Bega, on the first day. We would go all the way to Da'Juro where we'd camp in the empty house and be ready to receive our furniture early the next morning.

When we arrived at Bega, we had supper with Llewyn and Greer, but Rod was very eager to take possession of our new home, so he excused himself after the meal and went to the house to unload our bedding. Just as I was wondering why he hadn't turned on the lights, I heard him coming back. Although I had arranged for the power to be connected, there was no electricity at Da'Juro.

Greer invited us to stay but Rod declined. "Thank you, Greer, but by hook or by crook I'm sleeping in our new house, with or without electricity!"

Then Dane piped up, "I'm not going! I'm not going to sleep in the dark! And, there's no food in the fridge!"

So while Rod and I camped out in an empty, dark house, our practical son made himself very comfortable. It was just as well he did. The next day was bedlam!

We phoned the power supplier from Greer's house in the morning, and were told that we might have to wait for more than a week for the power to be connected. Greer said not to worry, she would call someone who could get things moving. Not long after, we heard the moving van making its way up the road. We all hurried through cool, misty rain over the paddock to Da'Juro to watch the van turn into our front gate and begin to negotiate our driveway, which ran down into a gully and then up to the house.

The van stopped in the gully. Rod looked at me uneasily as the movers climbed out. We hurried down the hill to speak to them. As we drew closer we could smell what the trouble was. They were quarreling, and they were very intoxicated. As we approached, they redirected their belligerence to Rod, claiming our driveway was too steep. After a torrent of abuse they refused to drive the truck any farther.

"Look, pal," Rod protested, "we've built a house up there! We've had a whopping great crane and cement trucks and loads of timber and bricks up this driveway! How do you reckon we got it there?"

But still they refused to drive up to the house.

"Well, what are you going to do?" Rod demanded, and to our dismay they began to unload our furniture into the wet paddock. I'd made the big mistake of paying these men in full before they left Brunswick.

Greer phoned a neighbor to ask for help and moments later we saw him driving toward us through the paddocks. Then, as he approached our gully, his truck slowed and sank to its axles in mud.

I tried to take stock. We might not have power for days, the movers were unloading our furniture into a paddock in misty rain, there was a truck stuck in our gully and now Rod was hauling luggage from our vehicle in search of a towrope.

Then I saw a delivery van turn into our gate and remembered I'd ordered a new washing machine. The driver of the van carefully negotiated his way around the moving van and pulled up to the house. I hurried after him and showed him where the laundry room was.

Greer reappeared then saying, "I'm off to work now but I've called a friend. Her two sons have been surfing but they're on their way home."

I was confused. We needed movers, not surfers!

Then I noticed a white truck approaching our front gate. Now what? It was the power supply people. Thank goodness—Greer's friend must have been able to do something.

"It won't fit, Mrs. Waites."

I turned to the man at my side who had spoken. He looked familiar but I couldn't remember who he was. I assumed he was referring to the truck about to turn into our gateway.

I said, "Oh yes, I'm sure that truck will fit through our gate."

The man shook his head. "No, the space in the laundry room is too small."

Oh, he means the washing machine! A quick check revealed that the space left for the washing machine was a few millimeters too narrow.

"Well, Mrs. Waites, can I shave the cupboards?"

He could have shaved his head for all I cared. I think I was hyperventilating. A few moments later he reappeared and exclaimed, "But Mrs. Waites, there's no power! I can't shave the cupboards without power."

An army of men in white overalls and white helmets spilled out of the newly arrived truck. "I think you'll have power, soon," I said.

The activity in the gully around our growing pile of furniture had increased. Rod had pulled the neighbor's truck out of the mud and together they were loading boxes onto it from the moving van. Cars had arrived, too, and I saw our leather lounge hurrying up the road on four bare legs.

"Hello, Mrs. Waites. I'm Caine and this is Ben. Where do you want it?"

I noticed their board-shorts—so these were the surfers. Bless their kind hearts and broad shoulders!

Then a big box appeared on two legs and a head popped over the top. "Hello, Mrs. Waites!" It was Nicholas, from next door, closely followed by his brother Damien, also carrying a box. I could have hugged them all! I was tearful with gratitude. Laughing and joking, these young men strode up and down the hill, moving our belongings out of the rain and into the house.

At the height of all this activity Ben came up to me with a torn, muddy rag. "Is this anything you need, Mrs. Waites?" he asked. "I was going to throw it in the trash but I thought you might want it."

It was the silk dress I'd bought for that year's Spring Racing Carnival at Flemington. It had a red top and a sweeping concertina skirt unfolding into drifts of red, tan, black and cream. The torn remnants waved in the breeze as if to farewell the life I'd left behind. There'd be no more spring racing carnivals, or executive entertaining. I'd be shopping for jeans and rubber boots now, and gardening gloves.

"No thank you, Ben, I don't need that. Put it in the trash."

It seemed hours since breakfast and I ached for a cup of coffee. We didn't even have a box of cookies to offer our helpers. Our car was part of the moving team so I couldn't go shopping. Then Greer reappeared with platters of sandwiches, cold drinks, hot drinks, mugs and cups.

Finally the power was connected, the washing machine installed between shaved cupboards, and our belongings were safely indoors. Greer shopped for our essential groceries and another neighbor made us a beautiful dinner. All these kind people made us feel so welcome.

During our final consultation with Dr. John, he had reminded me of the enormity, for Dane, of our move to the Bega Valley. He had suggested that we take it one step at a time, allowing Dane to become accustomed to the new house and surroundings before organizing work or any other activities for him. He was so right. We could see Dane struggling both physically and emotionally with his new environment. Moving from a narrow, inner-city terrace to this spacious house with its expansive views had a huge impact on me. How much bigger a change was it then for Dane for whom sights and sounds were so important? We'd grown accustomed to neighbors' conversations and laughter, and traffic noise. Now we woke to birdsongs and the mooing of cows. Now we had acres of bushland all to ourselves. Now all the trees around us were our trees!

Dane had great difficulty grasping all this. We progressed slowly and gently, not rushing anything, just as Dr. John had suggested. Dane coped with our moving-in day by withdrawing into his own space. We involved him by asking for help with the heavy furniture but we were conscious of his confusion. The following morning we sensed a bout of depression coming on. Rod deflected it quickly. "How about a walk at Tathra beach, Dane?" he suggested.

"Oh yes, Dad, that would be great!"

This spur-of-the-moment outing established a pattern for our first summer in the Bega Valley. Rod offered to unpack while I spent time with Dane but, knowing I'd never find anything afterward, I said I would rather do it. So for weeks father and son disappeared each day after breakfast and explored endless beaches, forests and countryside. When they came home, Dane would tell me about all the places they had discovered. This was ideal therapy for Dane. And for Rod! And it also helped them move to a deeper level of companionship.

Dane began to use his bedroom as more than just a place to sleep and change his clothes. By choice it was immaculately tidy. Ample shelving housed his CD player and television, tenpin bowling trophies and matchbox cars, magazines and photograph albums. Every day he would sit in his easy chair poring over albums and magazines. He began to take time out with a photo album each morning. This would help him organize his thoughts for the day ahead.

To this day, it is Dane's photograph albums that he enjoys most in the quiet of his own room. These albums allow him to slow his racing, confused thoughts. Whereas other young people might watch a video, he'll browse through photographs. Dane has acquired a library of photograph albums and uses each one at different times, depending on his mood or needs. If he's thinking of travel or vacations, he'll look through an album of a past trip. If he's feeling a bit down, he might find an album to remind him of happy occasions or helpful people. We'll hear him having discussions with his friend "Dane" as he examines the images.

He'll say, "Look, see how happy you were there, Dane? See, that's you—you're looking very calm and in control. Now isn't it better to be happy, Dane? So when you go to work tomorrow, you can be that happy person."

Each and every day of his life Dane steps from the silent withdrawal of autism into our confusing world. He must find his own path and devise his own signposts and cues. We can't do any of this for him but we can help him with photographs.

After a wonderful summer exploring the Bega Valley, Dane began to talk about starting work, so we re-established contact with Tulgeen. He decided to join the Work Crew, which operates indoors and outdoors, in town and out in the rural areas, wherever their contracts take them. This gave Dane the space he needed. The work also helped him develop a sense of belonging in his new environment. We'd be driving through the district and he'd proudly point out the grass he'd cut or the white posts he'd painted.

The supervisor encouraged Dane to use his initiative, and he began to notice when something needed to be done at home. We assumed his self-esteem would develop alongside his new skills but as usual nothing happened easily for Dane. As fast as his skills expanded his self-esteem diminished.

Dane's struggles were the result of his inability to deal with the differing personalities he encountered in the Work Crew. He has difficulty with "ownership of behavior." Should he overhear a dispute between two or more people, he'll think it's his fault.

Once we've identified a situation we've learned to ask, "Who owns the problem, Dane?"

He might reply, "It's Bob and Jim's problem, Mum."

So I'll ask, "Are you Bob?"

"No, Mum."

"Are you Jim?"

"No, Mum."

"So, who are you?"

"I'm Dane, Mum."

"Well, it's not your problem, is it?"

We need to remind him to ask himself, "What is Dane's identity?" and "Where do Dane's responsibilities begin and end?" I must encourage him to work through these questions and accept responsibility for his answers. This is working very slowly for him.

Sometimes he'll recognize a potential problem, and he'll say, "But that's not my problem, is it, Mum?"

"No, son," I'll answer. "That's not *your* problem."

Then he can relax. Sometimes he'll add, "We've all got problems, haven't we, Mum?"

"Oh, yes, Dane. We've all got problems."

Dane cannot fathom the difference between friendly banter and a genuine squabble. Nor can he understand when someone is joking. His father's mannerisms are very familiar to him, but he'll still flinch at a deadpan joke from Rod and check the expression on my face. If I'm smiling, he'll relax and exclaim, "Oh, Dad's joking! That was a pretend!"

Daily debriefing after Dane comes home from work became routine from this time. We do this by listening to his thinking aloud. This is the only way we can identify problems. We'll say, "I hope you don't mind, Dane, but I heard you thinking aloud and you were saying such-and-such. I think your friends might be joking about that."

His uncertainty has eased with time but situations still arise where he's left floundering. Is this a joke? Is it for real? Should the situation deteriorate, his self-esteem diminishes and he withdraws into himself. It's very difficult for us to help him then, and occasionally he becomes so withdrawn he's unable to respond to our efforts at all. Then we must say, "Well, Dane, let's move on and enjoy today. We'll deal with the problem when we can."

Rod's mother died not long after we moved to Bega. Earlier, when we had told Dane how ill his beloved Ga was, he had lashed out angrily, shouting, "Don't you tell me she's going to die or I'll scream and I'll scream and scream!"

So we were very surprised by his quiet, philosophical reaction to the news of her death. "Well, Mum, her body's in the ground but her spirit's in heaven, so that's all right."

On his grandmother's birthday, some time later, he said, "Today is Ga's birthday, Mum, so I hope God remembers to give her a birthday cake."

Dane has his own idea of heaven and I'm certain this gave him strength to draw upon when his beloved grandmother died. He still wonders if we can visit her. He finds it very difficult to accept that God doesn't share and that people cannot come back.

Dane's cycling ability bloomed when we moved to the country because he could ride to his heart's content. On Friday nights he'd unfold a road map and plan the weekend's ride. We would arrange to meet him at specific points, then we'd bring him home.

As Dane learned his way around, he wanted to explore farther afield. From time to time we'd have a weekend away. Dane could comfortably ride up to sixty miles in a day. After our first such excursion Dane was unusually articulate, almost poetic, as he described the clouds, colors and mountain views, and the vast distances.

On another occasion we agreed to accompany him up the Clyde Mountain to Braidwood. Rod and I drove up the Clyde ahead of Dane. As we twisted and climbed up the steep bends I protested that this was too much, that we'd have to stop and give Dane a lift. Rod disagreed vehemently, arguing that Dane would be mortified. So we drove on and waited at Braidwood.

This was the only time I have seen Dane absolutely exhausted after a ride. He couldn't speak! Later I asked, "Did you push your bike up the hills?" He was most offended. "No way, Mum. That's for wimps!"

One day we arranged to take the Harley and meet Dane for a picnic lunch. While Rod parked the bike I headed for the local pie shop. As I walked back to the picnic grounds I laughed at the sight of Rod's lanky, black-leathered frame atop a table in the otherwise deserted area. His stance clearly stated, "Our table, clear off!"

I teasingly suggested he didn't need to guard the table with his life, that with all those other empty tables no one was likely to want to share ours, but he just grinned at me. Then, as I was setting out our lunch, a small car pulled into the picnic grounds. Greeting us cheerfully—"Hello! Out for a ride on our motorcycle, are we?"—its occupants headed straight for our table, unpacked their picnic and arranged themselves around Rod as if he were an oversized centerpiece.

Then along came a second group in a big shiny four-wheel-drive vehicle: "Lovely day! Gee, I bet that bike goes fast!"

Rod's face was a picture of amazement as the first group cheerfully squeezed up to make room for the second. Craning their necks around him, the merry band of total strangers chatted away like old friends.

When Dane arrived on his bicycle, he gave his father a disapproving look. "Why are you sitting in the picnic, Dad?" he asked.

As soon as Dane heard about the fifty-kilometer Mallacoota Classic Bicycle Race, he wanted to do it. Rod took Dane to Mallacoota and drove him along the route of the race, carefully explaining what he should do in the event of a fall, or a puncture, or if the race became too much for him. On the morning of the race, Dane was very nervous. Rod was uneasy, too, but he didn't let Dane see this. He asked him if he really wanted to go ahead with the race. "It's no big deal if you back out." No way! Dane was determined to compete.

Not having a racing handicap, Dane was placed with a group of early starters. Rod's heart sank when he saw the other cyclists' state-of-the-art racing bikes. Anxiously he watched as Dane lined up on his mountain bike, took off at the sound of the starter's gun, and rode through the town and out of sight. Other competitors joined the race then, the professionals at the rear attracting the most attention.

Unpleasant scenarios began to play on Rod's mind as he walked around Mallacoota. What if Dane had a fall? Would he become disoriented and lose his way?

The professional riders roared home first. After this burst of excitement Rod positioned himself to await the amateurs. As the loudspeaker announced their imminent arrival he scanned the horizon with mild interest, thinking he wouldn't be seeing Dane for some time. To his utter astonishment there was Dane pedaling furiously over the crest of a hill and down the road: "All I could see was this huge smile on a bicycle. He was going for it, zooming through the finishing line. I'd hoped he'd just find his way back safely but he was finishing like a champion! The tears were pouring down my face; I was so proud and so thankful."

The riders gathered around afterward to relax with a cold drink. Without hesitation Dane joined them. He was a rider, too! They were laughing with him and patting him on the back: *We saw you out there on the highway! You were going for it, mate!* This gave Dane a huge sense of achievement. He arrived home that evening like an Olympic hero, and Erin was there with her family to share the triumph.

Some months later, when Rod asked Dane if he'd like to compete in the race the following year, he was surprised when Dane said no.

"Was it too hard, Dane?" Rod asked him.

"No, Dad, but I've done that race. I'll try something else now on the bike."

Rod was impressed. Been there, done that. Time to move on!

Despite the obvious benefits of cycling, the solitary nature of these excursions concerned us a little. So we were delighted when Llewyn Waters suggested Dane might enjoy running. Llewyn and Ray Ryan were planning to enter Sydney's City to Surf run. Would Dane like to join them when they trained? Yes, indeed he would!

It wasn't a daily routine. A couple of times a week they'd run along quiet country roads and enjoy a barbecue afterward. This camaraderie with all the usual banter and joshing was a new experience for Dane, but he learned to accept having his territory invaded in this way by people who were his friends. It really gave him a lift, being one of the boys.

Inevitably Dane became interested in the City to Surf run. Could he run in it too? We didn't know what to think. How could he cope with that massive crowd? On the other hand, if he could cope then what a wonderful experience it would be. Llewyn believed Dane could do it. We respected his judgment and tried to keep our own fearful imaginings in check.

So began our preparation. We collected photographs, magazine articles, anything we could find about the race, discussing it all with Dane. We sent off his entry form and in due course his race number arrived in the mail, with its stern reminder that no one could run in the race without this official identification. We made reservations at a hotel in Bondi and finally the great day dawned.

Ray Ryan joined us at the hotel for breakfast. He explained to Dane how he always felt a bit anxious before a City to Surf run because there was a huge crowd of runners. He talked about what they would do while they waited for the start because this seemed to take such a long time. This was all Ray's idea; he understood that Dane needed this preparation.

Llewyn and Ray wanted the morning to be unhurried for Dane so they left early to secure a good starting position at the front. Then they noticed Dane wasn't wearing his race number. It was too late to return to our hotel so after eventually finding the late entry booth they joined a long, slow line for a new number. As the time dragged on Llewyn knew they were losing any chance of a place at the front. At this rate they'd be boxed into the middle of the crowd, but they waited and eventually Dane had his new number.

The officials' supply of safety pins was exhausted so Llewyn and Ray began to remove pins from their own numbers to share with Dane.

Suddenly Dane piped up, "Mum packed some pins, Llewyn!"

Llewyn assumed the pins would be back at the hotel too but still he asked where I'd put them.

"On my running singlet!"

"What running singlet, Dane?"

Dane broke into a big smile and raised his windbreaker to reveal his original number pinned to a running singlet. The spare bunch of pins was safely attached to the singlet too!

No one had thought to ask Dane the direct question, "Do you have your number?" They had just looked at his windbreaker and assumed he'd left his number behind at the hotel.

Dane and his friends acquitted themselves admirably in the City to Surf. The distance presented no problems for Dane. In fact, after a shower and a light lunch, he swam laps in Bondi's pool until Rod and I became exhausted just watching him.

Afterward, I asked, "Dane, how did you cope, running with all those people?"

His answer astonished and gratified me. "Oh, it was easy, Mum. I just kept my head down and my eyes were watching my feet in front of me so I had my own space."

I wished Vicki Bitsika could have heard him say this. To me, Dane's explanation was a powerful endorsement of the "circles concept" and Vicki Bitsika's teaching strategies. Though I'm certain even Vicki could never have imagined him running with 42,000 people!

After the City to Surf run, Rod and I wondered if the Tathra to Bega Half Marathon fun run would be more like a social occasion for Dane. It was, but not as we'd expected! It hadn't occurred to Rod or me to explain the function of the drinks booths along the City to Surf route to Dane. So on the Tathra to Bega run he was astonished when, every few kilometers, yet another kind person stepped forward to offer him a drink of water. Each time this happened, Dane introduced himself politely before accepting the drink. He would then look around for a trash can in which to deposit the empty paper cup. He was horrified to see people snatching drinks without even saying hello and then throwing the used cups aside.

When Dane eventually pounded down the hill into Bega's main thoroughfare, a big smile on his face, he crossed the finishing line and threw his fists skyward. Spotting his father, he called out, "Did I win, Dad?"

Rod shook his son's hand and patted him on the back. "You didn't win the race, Dane, but you're a real winner!"

The black forest cake

We had hoped for some financial winners among our first drop of calves. The Dexter cattle had seemed like a good business proposition for Da'Juro so we had artificially inseminated a small herd of crossbred females as a first step toward breeding up to purebred animals. Naturally, we had hoped for heifer calves. Just a few heifers in the first year would have covered our establishment costs and an all-heifer calving would have been very profitable indeed!

The first calf to arrive was a bull, as was the second. Then as more bull calves appeared the first stage of our breeding program went out the window. This happened again in the second year, and once again in the third. Then we confronted Bega's worst drought in half a century.

Despite this, we have had no second thoughts about our decision to move to the country. The positive aspects of our new life have far outweighed the negative financial ones. Rod's health has improved and Dane has moved ahead in ways we had never imagined.

The responsibility of land ownership was a new experience for us. We learned about soil testing and noxious weeds, rabbit and fox control, and how to put up a strong, neat fence line. Rod and I enrolled in courses on beef cattle production and small-area farming. We diversified into alpaca wethers for their luxuriant fleeces and delightful personalities. They soothe us on troubled days and they're light eaters so we don't need extra fodder. We sell the fleece through a cooperative and the process is a delight for us all.

Mindful of Dr. John's recommendation that Dane become accustomed to his new environment before we introduced new elements, we delayed acquiring another dog, but eventually Shabuoth joined our family. She's a purebred Rhodesian ridgeback. *Shabuoth* is a Hebrew word meaning "festival of agriculture." Her breeder told us how early settlers in Africa used ridgebacks to raise the alarm against prowling lions. She's grown to the size of an average Great Dane. She's not an overly energetic lady, but her deep, resounding bark would make any stray lion think twice. Mostly, she's Dane's constant companion.

While Dane enjoyed the Work Crew and appreciated the support he received there, he was quick to recognize another opportunity. Shortly before his twentieth birthday he suggested we attend an open day at Workability, a local employment agency that helps job-seekers with a disability to secure and maintain employment.

When Dane introduced Rod and me to the manager of Workability, Virginia Fitzclarence, he said, "This lady will help me find a job, Dad. A real job!" His comment surprised us. We had always considered his job with the Work Crew as real work and had no idea he perceived it otherwise.

Dane became Workability's first client with autism. When Bega Valley Motors listed a vacancy for a part-time cleaner, Virginia agreed that Dane should apply. This was Bega Valley Motors' first experience with hiring a person with a disability. Virginia put forward two applicants; there was an interview and selection process as with any other job.

Rod attached a photograph of Dane in the country with his bike to his resumé. This gave Dane an opportunity to talk about something he was interested in at his interview, which made his disability less obvious. It also highlighted one of his skills, and he looked really good in the photograph. It was a terrific advertisement for him and he was given the job.

When Dane was first employed, he received full-time wages. However, because of his autism, he was unable to be fully productive and, although Bega Valley Motors were anxious to keep him on, they found it difficult to justify paying him a full-time salary. The staff at Workability suggested using the Supported Wage System (SWS) to resolve the situation. Dane was employed under the Vehicle Industry Repair Service and Retail Award. After lengthy negotiations on Dane's behalf, this award was varied to include the SWS component. Now, under the SWS, Bega Valley Motors remunerates Dane according to his annually assessed productivity level.

I worried how Dane would react to this busy car dealership with people coming and going, telephones ringing, a public address system barking messages and the normal banter of men in the workplace. However, I believed that if he knew exactly what he was expected to be doing every moment of each day he could cope. I wondered if the simple task list drawn up for Dane's work experience at the Caf could be adapted to suit his present needs.

In conjunction with his new employers, Virginia ascertained exactly what Dane would be expected to do and how long each task could be expected to take. With this information we compiled a simple duty statement, with starting and finishing times set down for each task. It became known as the "List" and copies were distributed to Dane, myself, his workplace supervisor and Workability support workers.

The List, which Dane continues to operate by today, deflects the very real threat of him having too many bosses. Only his immediate supervisor can alter it, in consultation with Workability. Using the List, Workability support workers monitor his productivity and behavior patterns without interruption, simply by calling at his workplace and checking his activity with the time of day. Other people have duty statements so for Dane there is no stigma attached to the List.

On the very rare occasion anyone asks him to carry out an unlisted task, he'll smile and agree but almost certainly not do it. Workmates, who have no idea that behind Dane's smile is confusion and distress, will joke about the tactics he uses to avoid such requests, saying things like, "Oh, he's so cunning, and lazy. He'll stay out of sight so he doesn't have to do the extra work." Cunning and laziness have nothing to do with it. It's not work that's unwelcome to Dane, it's change. Without careful preparation by the appropriate people, the slightest change in his routine can still ruin his day and, possibly, his entire week. At home he'll become anxious and depressed and spend hours in assertive self-talk trying to come to terms with the change at his workplace.

Another problem for Dane in the workplace is that it is easy for him to misinterpret another person's language. He'll take on board the expression in a person's voice before processing their words. If this upsets him he's likely to disregard their words altogether. For example, his supervisor might notice an overflowing bin and bark, "Dane, the bin!" Dane will become agitated but it won't occur to him to empty the bin. Unless the supervisor says, "Dane, empty the bin," he'll agonize over why this person was so horrible, and may need Workability's support to restore his routine. This is why, given the nature of Dane's disability, we are always going to need a support mechanism such as Workability in the background.

Dane was delighted when car detailing was added to his list of tasks, but then a problem developed. He would become so engrossed in the detailing work that be would begin to neglect his regular cleaning tasks. Then he'd sense the pending arrival of a support worker and disappear into the labyrinth of his workplace. How could we ensure that he attended to all the tasks on his list? A technique I discovered at an autism workshop pointed the way through this dilemma.

At this workshop I learned that a single-page, clearly printed "Social Story" could provide Dane with a tangible clue to understanding situations that to him, as a person with autism, may be confusing. He'll discuss a problematic situation with me, and then together we'll find the right words to create his Social Story. Dane will print these words on a single page of paper and this "story" will become a prompt for him to respond in a socially acceptable manner. He can use his Social Story as a reminder of exactly what it is that might worry him and as a guide to how he can deal with the problem

Before I discovered the Social Story technique, I used newspaper clippings, magazine cuttings and photographs to try to explain issues to Dane. Social Stories, however, can be devised to suit Dane's specific needs. If necessary, they can be illustrated with computer-generated photographic images of real people.

Dane now has a folder of prepared Social Stories covering various contingencies. The following extract is from a story that helps Dane overcome his difficulty in changing from weekend activities to work on Monday mornings, and it also helps him to follow his list. He has named it "A Time for Work and A Time for Interests":

Not everybody has an interesting life. I have an interesting life. Many people don't have a job. They don't get paid. They get bored. I do have a job. I get paid my wage each week. I don't get bored. I am paid to do all the work on my list. I am paid to finish my list and do a good job. When I finish work for the day I can do

other things, like sports. Mum has to follow her list. If
Mum did not follow her list, who would cook the meals,
do the washing and keep the house nice for her family?
When Mum finishes her list she can do other things,
like reading.

For Dane, Social Stories convert his own words into reality. He creates and takes ownership of a Social Story, and when he reads it again it gives him a mechanism to work with. For months, Dane studied "A Time for Work and A Time for Interests" every Monday morning to remind him why he wanted to work and why he must follow his list. This story also reminds him that after work he can go to the gym, or for a run, or ride his bike.

When helping Dane compose a Social Story, I must remember to use more positives and fewer negatives. It needs to be in the first person: "I will," "I can." It must *belong* to Dane. If he's anxious on a Monday morning I'll suggest he read his Social Story before work. If he's very anxious he might say, "No, I don't want to read it." He'll say this because he knows that having read the story, he takes ownership of the information. The words are his. The information belongs to him: *Once I read that Social Story, I really do have to get back on track.* (The List works for him in the same way. He knows that once a support worker asks why he's not following his list, he has to take ownership of the situation: *Once I look at the List, I'm responsible.*)

Each Social Story must have a beginning and an end. Dane's whole day will fly out of control without the security of a known beginning and ending. Remove the controlling bookends and the whole row of books will topple over.

It's only in more recent years that we have properly recognized Dane's intense dislike of change.

One day I asked him, "Do you recall your terrible screaming when the lights turned red on our way to the Children's Hospital?"

Yes, he remembered.

"Do you remember why you screamed?"

"Yes. I just wanted the car to keep going."

It was so simple. I guess that's why he screamed in his stroller when I paused on our marathon walks. He hated the change from moving to stopping. He just wanted that stroller to keep going.

I asked him about his obsession with straight lines. "Why did you enjoy following the straight lines, Dane? Why did they have to be straight lines?"

He said, "They don't change, Mum. I can see where they go."

In other words, straight lines were predictable.

At a recent art exhibition Dane was studying a startling contemporary painting. He prefers photorealism so I was puzzled until it dawned on me that this abstract image was painted mostly in black.

"Do you remember how you always painted in black when you were young?" I asked him.

Dane didn't hesitate. "Oh yes, Mum, I remember."

"Do you remember why you painted in black?"

"Oh yes! Black was finished! You don't see through with black."

So that's why Dane preferred black. Black didn't change. Unlike other colors, black wasn't translucent; nor did black-on-black produce an unexpected third color.

Dane's earlier violent reactions to change have diminished into a gentler preference for sameness. His obsessive tidiness reflects this; he enjoys looking at his belongings but touches only those he uses regularly, such as his photograph albums. If I move something, he'll exclaim, "You've been mucking around in my room, Mum!" He'll immediately notice the slightest change in our surroundings, such as a fallen tree or an altered signpost. As a child without speech such changes would have provoked outbursts of screaming. Now he'll simply remark on the fallen tree, or ask why the signpost is different.

We assumed we'd celebrate Dane's coming of age with a handful of guests at a restaurant, but Dane announced he wanted a party at home. It never occurred to us that the boy who screamed if two or more people walked through our front door would want his twenty-first birthday party at home. It hadn't occurred to Dane that it should be anywhere else!

Rod and I prepared a list of friends and relatives. We read this through with Dane and asked him who he remembered and who he would like to invite. His face lit up. "Oh, *all* these people, please!"

We then asked him to give us the names of his friends from work and the gym and from Tulgeen, and the list grew longer and longer. Eventually we mailed ninety-five invitations. Dane's birthday fell on a public holiday weekend, so our most optimistic hope was that half of those invited would come. In no time at all we had received ninety-three acceptances!

Dane asked for a barbecue, which simplified the catering. We emptied the workshop to accommodate a disco. Early winter can be chilly in Bega, so Rod converted a forty-four gallon drum into a brazier, which he set up outdoors with seats and a few tons of firewood.

Need I have asked what color theme Dane wanted?

"Oh, black please, Mum! I'd like black balloons and black streamers and black cakes and black cutlery and black everything!" He even knew where to buy black disposable cutlery and plates in Bega.

Tactfully, Rod suggested a black and white theme—"for Collingwood"—and Dane agreed.

My imagination froze on the idea of a black cake. "But you can't have black cake, Dane," I said.

"Yes I can, Mum! Black forest cake!"

So we had black and white balloons, streamers, cutlery and crockery. Margaret brought black-and-white check tablecloths for every flat surface inside and outside the house. Rod bought new black stock troughs to serve as ice buckets. They looked very effective and our cattle use them now— black cattle, of course.

Dane's guests came from all over Australia. They mingled happily outside and inside, in the disco and around the fire. Dane danced and talked and scarcely drew a breath all evening. Rod made a heartfelt, beautiful speech. Proudly Dane stood next to his Dad, Erin by his side. I said a few words and Dane made a short speech. Then other guests spoke. I remember in particular one young man's concluding words. He said, "Well, he's just Dane. He's our mate and we all love him."

Then the gym crew began to call, "Come on, Sorrensen! Time to cut the cake!" (Dane's nickname is borrowed from renowned Australian athlete Dane Sorrensen.) Thanks to our local baker we had an enormous, beautifully decorated black forest cake. This was sliced and distributed and the young men began calling out again. "Time to open the presents! Come on, Sorrensen, open the presents!"

We hadn't planned for Dane to open his gifts in this big noisy crowd. Memories of a seven-year-old who wouldn't unwrap his present from Santa made us unsure if he'd cope. I could see my worry that he might lose control mirrored in Margaret's eyes, but then Rod did something that helped me relax. He slid a very large present out of Dane's sight. I guessed he hoped that if Dane did become overwrought, this extra-large gift would appeal to his liking for big and help him settle down.

Dane read each card and carefully unwrapped each gift. He was obviously delighted with every one. The young men from the gym cheered as Rod finally produced the extra-large gift. Dane just beamed. The young men understood his love of anything big and as Dane accepted the present they began clapping and chanting, "Huge, huge, huge!" Soon all the guests were stomping and clapping and shouting, "HUGE! HUGE! HUGE!" The noise was overwhelming as Dane slowly removed the paper. Margaret caught my eye and shook her head. I was fearful, too—Dane had never experienced anything like this. And yet in those moments of joyous mayhem we saw Dane in a new light. In this crowd of people in his space, in this hullabaloo of stamping and clapping and chanting, he was coping like a champion!

I wondered what the enormous present could contain. The chanting reached a crescendo as Dane removed the final wrapper. I was stunned. Knowing how Dane loves photographs, these young men had organized a framed collage of photographs taken at the gym, and a head-and-shoulders enlargement of Dane with his weights. If I'd racked my brains for months, I couldn't have chosen a better gift.

When the party was over, I stepped outside and saw Dane and one of his cousins relaxing side-by-side on a bench. They were chatting quietly and gazing into the fire, the flames illuminating their faces. I saw her rest her head against Dane's arm. Dane didn't flinch or attempt to move away from her. He simply placed his arm around her shoulder, as if to welcome her into his "hug circle."

For years Dane had been the one who hung back at family parties, unwilling and unable to socialize. As a child he had known family was special, but he never really grasped what this meant. He didn't understand emotional bonds. Now I could see that he did. We were so grateful that Rod's sisters had brought their families the long distance to be with us.

I did enjoy the Hilton

The Cluny Sisters are Dane's second family. He has loved and trusted these women for most of his life. He responds to their compassion, to their enjoyment of Cluny's beautiful gardens and to their quiet daily routine. In turn, they say he brings with him a great-to-be-alive feeling. Margaret describes his ability to make other people feel good: "I've never known Dane to say anything negative about anyone. I'll sometimes joke with him, saying, "I'm growing old now Dane." He'll smile at me and say, "No you're not, Margaret! You're not old. You're still young!" He'll say this to the elderly, too. He always lifts their spirits." Cluny Convent operates a hostel for older people. Dane always enjoys talking to them, listening to music and watching television with them.

The contemplative environment of the convent appeals to Dane. Margaret recognized this very early on: "He's always content to share a companionable silence. I believe few people have this beautiful gift. This tranquility follows Dane when he accompanies me to our chapel. We'll say a prayer, then of his own accord he'll move forward and kneel at the altar. I can see that he's really in touch with God. There's a real presence there—God's presence."

Cluny Hostel is where Dane wants to live when the time comes. He keeps safe a copy of a letter from the Superior General, Sister Marie-Noel Lefrancois, confirming the Order's invitation for him to do this, and verifying the arrangements. From time to time he will say to me, "That's where I'm going to live, Mum, when I'm older." It's a blessing to hear these words. Many parents of children with special needs must often make plans without knowing what their son or daughter really wants.

Dane met Sister Marie-Noel Lefrancois when she visited Melbourne. She'd sit beside him at mealtimes and, through an interpreter, tell him about Paris. "Paris!" she'd say. "Oh, Dane, you should come over and visit us in Paris!" Of course Dane takes statements like this literally. To him the Superior General's invitation was set in stone. So he began saving his wages to go to Paris.

An invitation to visit the Order's Mother House is extended to all Cluny Sisters after they have been some years in the congregation. Margaret always chose to visit her family in Fiji, but after Dane's twenty-first birthday, she asked if Dane could go with her to Paris. A letter was sent to Sister Marie-Noel who wrote back to say that Dane would be most welcome. Dane had been saving hard, and Rod and I agreed that as a twenty-first birthday gift we'd make up the difference.

The plan was that Margaret and Dane would vacation together, and then Dane would return home while Margaret went on retreat. "Preparing" the airline for Dane's outward Melbourne to London flight was eased by our friend in Customer Service, though Dane was very concerned that, with no direct Melbourne–Paris flights, they'd need to use Qantas to London and British Airways from London to Paris. He cross-examined us at length. Was British Airways safe?

Were their planes as clean as Qantas planes? Was the food as good as Qantas? Were the attendants polite?

Making the arrangements for Dane's unaccompanied return flight was almost overwhelming. Eventually, however, a plan was drawn up whereby airport staff would meet his plane from Paris at Heathrow and transfer him to his flight for Melbourne. Window seats were allocated and everything that could be pre-arranged was in place. Dane had no concerns about flying alone. He looked forward to that.

As we watched our slim, gentle friend walk through the departure gates beside her lofty, robust godson, we wondered if we were crazy or just naïve. For a moment I ached to run after them and beg them not to go. How on earth would Margaret manage if something went terribly wrong? Rod just shook his head: "Heavens above, are those two really going to Paris?"

Margaret phoned from the Mother House to tell us that they were tired and happy and that the long flight passed without incident. The Mother House stands in the heart of Paris, close to the Bastille Monument and Notre Dame Cathedral. It is a beautiful building in the traditional chateau style, built around a central courtyard. Dane and Margaret shared a suite of two bedrooms and a bathroom. Dane's room overlooked a park filled with trees; the sisters knew he'd enjoy that.

Margaret and Dane explored every place of interest in and around Paris. We have two photograph albums filled with their wonderful memories. Dane thoroughly enjoyed the food and the wine. For breakfast they'd have huge bowls of milky coffee with fresh baguettes and jam. They shared their dinners with the sisters or ate in a quieter area if Dane needed his space. Later, when Dane came home and people asked him if he'd had problems understanding the French, he said, "Oh no, the French people, they were great! I would just say "Oui, merci" and then we'd all laugh together!"

Dane and Margaret attended a very special celebration in the lovely Cluny Chapel when a number of young sisters from around the world were professed and received into the congregation. They arrived together for this service. Margaret moved into a pew halfway up the aisle, expecting Dane to sit beside her, but he walked to the front to sit with the young sisters and Sister Eucharia. The service was long and Sister Eucharia was concerned about Dane, but when she asked him about this after the ceremony, he said, "I enjoyed it, Sister Eucharia. That's where I wanted to be."

Dane established a rapport with the young sisters. His knowledge of maps helped him to understand where they came from. Sister Eucharia always gave the young sisters one-hour English lessons after dinner. One evening she knocked on Margaret's door quite late. She was eager to tell Margaret about her long conversation with her students. They had asked many questions about autism and Dane and his experiences. They told her how they felt good to be in a congregation that allowed this young man to come within the cloister, to be a guest in the Mother House. These young women returned to their communities throughout the world with valuable first-hand awareness of autism.

Unbeknown to Dane I'd written him a card and tucked it into his luggage. I wrote, "Congratulations, Dane! You've made it to Paris. Release this balloon with joy!" Margaret's photograph of Dane at the open casement window captures the moment when he released his very own red balloon to fly away to little Pascal. His expression, she told us, as he watched it drift over the Paris rooftops was quite wistful.

Dane's return flight was due before dawn but we arrived at the airport with time to spare. Flashing indicator boards said

QF10, Dane's flight, would be first to land. We'd arranged for him to be assisted through customs, so we positioned ourselves at the barrier directly opposite the sliding doors, expecting he'd be one of the first passengers to emerge. We clung to the barrier and to each other as the crowd jostled around us. The flashing lights changed—QF10 had landed! Rod gripped my hand tightly. Any minute, now! I was struggling not to cry.

Dane was not the first to come through the door. Nor the second, nor the third. We watched every passenger from that flight walk out of the customs hall. I didn't realize we'd begun watching passengers from the next flight until Rod spotted their different luggage tags.

We knew Dane needed our help behind those doors. I suggested Rod stay put in case he appeared and I'd run upstairs to the administration counter. I'd tried to "check in" with administration when we'd first arrived, but understandably the counter was unattended at 2.15 a.m. I ran across the concourse and up the escalator thinking how Dane would be tired and any problems at this stage could blow out of all proportion. Oh, the relief when I saw a real live person behind the counter! I rushed past the other people heading in the same direction.

Speaking slowly and clearly and trying not to gasp for air, I explained that Mr. Dane Waites, a young man with special needs on Flight QF10 from Heathrow, was almost certainly delayed in customs and could his father go to the customs hall right now, please, and help him?

The clerk scanned her computer screen and, to my intense relief, turned to me and smiled. Then she said, "Mr. Dane Waites wasn't on Flight QF10."

My knees almost buckled. I assured her our contact in Paris would have advised us of even the smallest change. "Maybe he's listed as Thwaites? Or maybe they've run the Dane into the Waites?"

Her smile faded. "I'm looking at the list and I'm telling you, he did not come in on that flight."

"Then please," I begged, "where is he? Where is my son?"

"I wouldn't have a clue where he is," she replied. "Maybe he's changed his plans. You'll have to contact him and ask him yourself."

She's finished with you, lady. Move aside, said the line of shuffling feet behind me. Sheer terror for Dane glued me to the floor. I imagined him lost at Heathrow or heaven knows where; fearful, cold and hungry; perhaps on the verge of losing control. *Stay very calm, speak clearly, breathe deeply. Maintain your dignity.* "I know others are waiting, but my son has special needs. Your computer has all the information. If he's lost at Heathrow, then it's your responsibility to find him. And I'm waiting right here until he's found!"

Taken aback, the clerk asked where Dane was staying.

"It's in your files. Please look at your screen," I said.

More shuffling of feet. Reluctantly, she began clicking through files. "Oh, yes. There's quite a lot here."

As if I didn't know that!

"But it doesn't say where your son is now."

I wanted to shake this person. Instead I begged, "Then please let's speak to someone who can help. Right now! I'm finding it very hard to stay calm."

I wondered what on earth Rod must have been thinking downstairs at the barrier. At last a supervisor appeared and ushered me behind a glass partition. "Bear with me, Mrs. Waites, and I'll make some phone calls."

I sat down and he made the call. Suddenly I heard, "Oh, he was in London!" Then he said to me, "It's all right, Mrs. Waites. We've found him, more or less."

More or less! I almost jumped out of the chair. It appeared Dane's flight from Paris had been delayed by a storm and had missed the connecting flight. The supervisor told me that he would have been put up in a London hotel for the night.

"And how is he getting back here?" I asked.

"Oh, he'll have boarded another flight by now."

The room began to spin.

"Are you absolutely certain he's been escorted onto another flight? Are you certain he's not waiting in a hotel room? I must remind you, my son has special needs."

The supervisor looked at me in astonishment. "Really? Special needs!"

"Yes, special needs. The data is there in front of you."

He began to look at the computer screen. *Click, click.* He shook his head. *Click, click.* "There is a lot of data here, Mrs. Waites. A lot of data."

"Yes, I know. Please keep looking. Please!"

More clicking and finally his face brightened. "Now I understand your concern!" he exclaimed. "Here's the information."

The computer revealed that a flight attendant had checked Dane into a London hotel where he'd stayed overnight. The attendant had checked him out of the hotel the following day, and onto his Melbourne flight where he'd been placed in the same attendant's care. It was all so easy.

My head pounded as I groped my way downstairs. Rod was glued to the barrier in the distance. I beckoned him to come to me but he shook his head. He wasn't giving up his spot.

I pushed my way through the crowd to Rod. Peeling his fingers off the barrier, I tried to explain why I'd spent all that time unearthing a perfectly straightforward explanation. As we tottered off to the restrooms, Rod kept glancing over his shoulder. "No, Rod, he's not coming today. He's still on his way."

We returned to the motel where we'd stayed the previous night and almost broke our noses against the glass doors.

A cleaner stared at us glumly, mouthing words through the glass. Then the receptionist appeared with a key.

"Hello," I said. "Nice to see you again. You've accidentally locked the door, have you?"

"Oh no," she replied. "I've just arrived. We don't open the doors till seven thirty."

She looked somewhat puzzled when I asked if it was seven thirty in the morning. I don't think we knew what day it was, let alone what time. It felt like mid-afternoon to me.

Rod made another reservation. "Could we please have a room for another day, or two, or perhaps three?"

We resumed our dawn vigil the next day. What would the morning bring? A joyous reunion or a noisy tantrum? Would Dane have lost control on the plane? Indicators blinked the message that his flight had landed. Gripping the barrier, we stared at the sliding doors. Five minutes passed. We were rigid with trepidation. Ten minutes. The first passenger appeared, then the second. Then there was Dane, striding toward us, all smiles and hugs and kisses!

Rod interrupted my small talk to ask Dane about luggage.

Dane shrugged, "Oh, they've lost that, Dad." Then he turned toward a person standing nearby and said, "But don't worry. This lady says they'll find it."

A smiling flight attendant extended her hand. "Dane has been a wonderful passenger."

We tried to tell her how grateful we were, and then she left. As she walked away, Dane appeared uneasy. "Mum, the lady's going now."

"Yes, Dane, she's going now. She's on duty and has to finish her work."

"Yes, Mum, but she's *going!*"

"It's all right, Dane, she's done her job now. It's all right!"

Dane wasn't convinced but Rod and I were anxious to sort out the question of the lost luggage. The luggage clerk tapped a keyboard and asked for Dane's passport.

Dane looked at me and said, "Mum, I was trying to say when the lady was going—she's got my passport!"

The clerk interrupted, "Don't worry, sir. What's the lady's name?"

Dane looked crestfallen. "I don't know her name. We weren't introduced."

The clerk began to direct us upstairs to administration. "There's a counter . . . ."

"Yes, I know where it is. Thank you."

We explained our problem, a message blared through the public address system and the passport was retrieved. After a third night at the same motel we collected Dane's luggage.

Later I asked Dane, "How did you manage in the plane, during the storm? Goodness, *I* would have been so nervous. How did *you* feel?"

Without hesitation he said, "Oh, Mum, it was all right. I didn't get upset. It was a terrific storm, Mum. One lady, she really lost her brain! And the poor attendant, but it wasn't his fault!"

He described how, after the storm, he'd been taken to the cockpit. The co-pilot had offered to telephone us, but Dane knew we'd be driving to Melbourne by then. "I told him you'd wait, Mum. I said my mum and dad would wait and wait and wait for me!"

He had taken the unexpected stopover in his stride, too. "I stayed in a wonderful hotel, Mum, I'll have to take you there one day. It's called the Hilton. Oh, I did enjoy the Hilton!"

Hold that paddle

As a person receiving services from a government-funded organization, Dane is entitled to an Individual Service Plan, or ISP. In Dane's case, ISP meetings are arranged by Workability, supervised by a coordinator and attended by Dane and other people of his choice. At each meeting listed agenda items insure Dane's requests and plans are recognized and acknowledged. These items relate to health, home living, wages and savings, vacations, community access, transport, education and leisure activities.

Dane recognizes the value of these meetings. He knows that without strong support and input from involved, caring people, the quality of life for people with a disability is generally diminished. Occasionally, the results of Dane's ISP meetings can only be described as spectacular.

It was at an ISP meeting, when Dane was twenty-two, that he first expressed serious interest in acquiring his driver's license. Years before he had asked if he could drive the car when he grew up and at the time we had explained that, like everything else, he'd need to take this in stages, and thus a long, long process began. First we had worked on his understanding of the road rules, gently drawing his attention to these when we were driving: "That driver made a mistake. Can you tell us what he should have done, Dane?"

He began to observe and comment: "Well, Dad, that driver's not doing the right thing, is he? He should have indicated left." Over a period of at least seven years, he developed a growing awareness of the road rules and driver responsibility. Occasionally Rod would take him to a private road where he could safely take the wheel. At Da'Juro we bought a four-wheel-drive bike to negotiate steep hills and gullies and after a number of lessons Dane could ride this bike to his heart's content. Simple tasks such as ferrying the trash container to the main road for collection honed his skills and gave him a sense of purpose.

However, I admit my heart sank when Dane raised the matter of his learner-driver's permit at the ISP planning meeting. I envisioned hours of repetitive work but his ISP coordinator was very positive, suggesting Dane work with the "Roadtester" computer software.

After months of work with his helper, Dane failed twice to obtain his learner's permit. But he just kept on trying. His helper believed he could do it, and eventually he did. I'm certain passing this test was the proudest achievement of Dane's life. We celebrated at dinner that evening with a huge mud cake with bright yellow icing and a big black "L." Now, with his "L" plates proudly attached to our car, Dane was ready to start driving on public roads.

In the months after Dane obtained his "L" plates, we treated ourselves to two vacation packages. With his behavior becoming more predictable now, we felt more confident about planning family vacations. We were learning to choose accommodation that catered for his need for space, and for his daily thinking aloud.

The first vacation was a dream come true for Dane. He and I went with Margaret to Dream World, Movie World, Sea World and all the other worlds that he'd heard about on the Gold Coast. I had booked an apartment with an ocean view. That was our only stipulation: that we must have a balcony

consulted with the patient. I'm not used to speaking with the parents."

I realized then that the doctor needed reassurance from Dane that he wanted improved eyesight, that this wasn't just something his mother and father wanted. So when the doctor asked if we had any more questions, I redirected his query to Dane who said, "Can you help me to see better?" Emphatically the doctor replied, "Yes!"

Immediately Dane and the doctor began to communicate, everyone relaxed, and a date was set for the operation. Dane's excellent memory allowed him to retain every detail of the procedure, outlined on a video the doctor showed us. The only problem we could foresee was that he would have to remain absolutely still for twenty seconds, eyes unmoving, while the procedure took place.

Dane has no concept of a time span. He can read the time on his watch, but if I ask him to come home in half an hour, he might return in five minutes or in three hours. However, if I ask him to be home in the same time it takes him to cycle to Merimbula and back—two hours—there's a good chance he'll be home in exactly two hours. He can relate time to distance traveled, but twenty seconds lying on his back and staring at a tiny light might be two seconds or twenty minutes to Dane.

So we began earnest role-playing. *Dane, count to twenty! Let's pretend you're having the procedure. Let's pretend you're lying down and looking at the light. Don't blink! Don't move! Now, count to twenty!* Rod would hold the stopwatch and we'd chorus the seconds from one to twenty.

We were grateful Dane was the day's first patient and wouldn't need to witness other people's reactions. From our chairs outside the surgery we could hear the specialist talking him through the procedure one more time, very clearly and precisely. Meanwhile Rod and I were a mess! We knew only too well what would happen should anything go wrong.

We'd arranged for Dane to have both eyes corrected. The doctor would attend to the first and if he felt comfortable, he'd do the second immediately. Otherwise we'd make another appointment or review the situation. We heard the machine and its twenty seconds of clicks. We held our breath. We waited, and waited, and then we heard a second series of clicks. What a relief! Dane wouldn't have to go through all this again. Nor would we!

Dane was a model patient. He desperately wanted this surgery to succeed. After the procedure he took meticulous care of his eyes. He wore his protective eye-shields and showered carefully. The results were outstanding. Dane still enjoys the vast improvement. Even now he'll pick up a familiar object and examine it closely as if he's seeing it for the first time. "Look," he'll exclaim. "No squinting!"

The big bike ride

With improved eyesight Dane became a more confident learner-driver. By this stage he knew all the road rules. It was practical experience he needed now. Rod agreed to teach him everything but forward and reverse parking. He left this to a professional.

We were introduced to a driving instructor who we believed would understand Dane's special needs. He was precise in his demands and, of course, Dane responded well to this. He obeyed instructions without question and learned the art of forward and reverse parking in only a few lessons.

We approached Dane's practical driving slowly and waited until *he* indicated his readiness to go for his license. When he did, the instructor arranged for a designated special-needs testing officer to conduct the test.

Taking his driving test was a big step into the unknown for Dane. We knew he was capable and that he knew all the road rules, but we didn't know if he would be able to interpret what would be asked of him and respond accordingly. We tried to prepare him for a host of eventualities—this might happen, that might happen. We tried to think of every possibility.

The big day arrived and naturally Dane was apprehensive. Rod waited with him for the visiting testing officer to arrive. They waited. And waited. The testing officer didn't arrive. This was the only contingency for which we hadn't prepared. It was a dreadful anti-climax.

The instructor arranged another reservation and a few weeks later Rod and Dane set off again. We assumed this specially designated testing officer would be a quietly spoken, compassionate individual. Both Rod and Dane almost jumped from their chairs in fright when a voice bawled, "Waites!"

Dane identified himself politely to the instructor.

"Got your car?" the man grunted.

Dane replied, "Yes, in the parking lot," adding quietly as an afterthought, "you might like to know it's the blue Jeep."

Rod was on the edge of a nervous collapse when Dane eventually returned to the RTA reception area. "Well, Dane? What did he say?"

Dane replied, "He told me to wait here, Dad."

"Did he say if you passed?"

"No, Dad, he just said to wait."

So they waited and waited.

Almost half an hour later another "Waites!" shot them to their feet.

The tester extended his hand to Dane, saying, "I couldn't fault you. Well done!"

Dane shared his wonderful news with Erin when he phoned her that evening for her birthday. Erin was over the moon. "Oh Dane, you're so independent!" It's very important for them both to be independent. They admire this quality in each other and in others. Erin often says to him, "Dane, you've got a job. That's being independent."

Later that same evening Dane produced a glossy brochure for the latest Honda Integra. "Look, Dad, I've ordered one of these."

Rod paled. The next morning he hurried off to find the salesman Dane had named. He thanked him for the brochure and said, "Can we talk about this?" When the salesman laughed and said, "It's okay, Rod, I haven't placed the order yet," Rod replied, "Could you hold off for a few years, please? Or maybe a few decades?"

Later we did buy a smart new Subaru hatchback in which Dane feels a sense of shared ownership. It's black—still his favorite color—and we didn't need a second mortgage to get it.

Having his provisional license boosted Dane's self-esteem. Proudly he'd say, "I'll take you for a drive, Mum!"

Within days of Dane becoming a provisional driver, we were stopped by a police breathalyser unit. "Just doing a breath check, driver, have you had a drink today?"

Dane looked puzzled. "But I'm on my P plates!"

"I see that, driver, but do you mind just telling me if you've had a drink today?"

Dane was highly offended. "But I'm on my P plates!"

The officer glared at him. "But-have-you-had-a-drink-today-driver?" he said slowly and deliberately.

Dane was emphatic. "No. You don't drink when you're on your P-plates!"

The officer heaved a sigh. "Well, do you object to taking a test?"

Dane had no objection! And he was delighted to show his license too. He'd show this to anybody any old time but he didn't appreciate any inference that he might have broken the rules. As we drove away he exclaimed, "Wasn't that a waste of time!"

When Dane heard about the RTA Big Bike Ride, a nine-day ride from Tamworth to Newcastle, he wanted to go on it. He raised the subject at his next planning meeting and to my surprise the coordinator suggested he leave the matter with her. When she spoke to us later she said, "I'm going on that bike ride. I'd be happy to help with his tent and be there for him." We asked if she knew what she was getting herself into. "Oh yes," she said. "It would be my pleasure to do this."

Within days Dane was in serious training. He was riding off into the unknown, so we couldn't prepare him. This was a worry for us, but he would say, "I can do this," so we had to trust his judgment.

The RTA Big Bike Riders can choose to fundraise for multiple sclerosis research so we explained to Dane what this meant and how the money is used, and he decided he wanted to do it. So Cluny Convent, Irabina Autistic Centre, Bega Valley Motors, the gym and Workability drew up sponsor lists for him. With this support Dane raised over six hundred dollars on his first RTA ride.

Dane phoned us regularly over the nine days. One day he was almost over the moon as he described a balloon ride he'd taken at Cessnock.

Rod and I drove to Newcastle to see him cross the finishing line. On the final day the riders released a cloud of balloons as they crossed Newcastle's Stockton Bridge. We saw two balloons tied to Dane's bike as he flashed over the finishing line. He is now totally convinced that balloons are for special occasions.

Dane selected a thank-you card for the friend who accompanied him on the ride. Inside he printed, "Dear Mary. Thank you for your company. It was a great bike ride. Happy days. Dane."

When he heard that the Big Bike Ride was an annual event, there was no doubt in his mind that he wanted to join the next one. The ride is a social event with no competitive pressure. It offers a routine that Dane learned quickly: *This is the breakfast line, here are the showers, here are the toilets, we'll be in Cessnock tonight and tomorrow we'll ride in a balloon.* It suits his need for structure and his love of open spaces.

Mary offered to help again, but we knew that now we must become involved, too. Thus began an exchange of letters, phone calls, forms and faxes. The RTA organizers had never had to deal with the needs of riders with autism. Once again, the computer didn't understand—support vehicles weren't allowed. I explained that we only needed to access the camp-site to put up and take down Dane's tent, and thankfully a most obliging young man eventually sorted it all out.

The 1998 RTA Big Bike Ride took us along the Murray River through the Riverina towns of Wakool, Mathoura, Moama, Deniliquin, Finley, Mulwala and Howlong, to Albury. This route could have been tailored just for Dane, and for us! We'd never have dreamed we'd enjoy the Murray River again so soon and in this manner.

Each morning Rod and I dismantled Dane's campsite and drove to the next stopover. We'd meet Dane exactly three hours after he'd left that morning's camp. Why three hours? There were no rules to state that a rider must finish within three hours. This was Dane's need for sameness reasserting itself. On the first day of his first ride he took three hours to cycle from the starting line to that evening's camp. So now on each RTA ride he aims to cycle between campsites in three hours, regardless of weather or terrain!

A few months after that year's bike ride, Dane received an invitation from some cyclists he'd met to join them for a reunion at Bundanoon. Words cannot express how much it means to Rod and me that such caring people chose to have Dane as their friend. This remarkable group included an outgoing, strikingly auburn-haired young woman named Helen Pitt. A journalist, she wrote this about her new friend:

A picture from the local newspaper of champion weightlifter Dane Waites hangs by a magnet on my refrigerator. Each day I go to get milk for my coffee, Dane stares back at me, huge smile, rippling muscles and an enormous medal hanging around his neck. Many visitors ask me who the Olympic champion is on my fridge. Friends joke he's the best-looking boyfriend I have ever had. I'm sure if I told Dane, he'd reply in the earnest way he does: "Yes, that's right."

I first met Dane in a pub in a place called Wakool in southern NSW. He was drinking a long cold lemonade, and his cheeks were ruddy from the crackling fire rather than a day on the bike. I had no idea he was autistic. He was just like all of us—another sweaty, smelly, and hungry bike rider.

Dane has become something of a legend on the annual Bicycle NSW RTA Big Rides. Since 1997, he has joined 1500 other cyclists on the organized cycling tour whose route varies each year. The year I met him we were cycling along the Murray.

His friends from Bega took turns accompanying Dane on the road. It is not a hard job—Dane charms most people he meets—the difficult part is keeping up with their charge. That goes for all of us. His energy and enthusiasm is well-known among bike riders. Dane is legendary not just for his cycling ability (he's often the first into camp) but also his dancing ability (he's always last off the dance floor). His gentle ways, his distinctive laugh and his love of life are contagious.

His parents Junee and Rod are well-known to bike riders too. Each day they meet Dane at the end of the ride, put up his tent, then whisk him off for a quiet time. Once it was a ride in a glider from Tocumwal, another time it was a ride on a Murray paddle steamer. It is clear his loving parents take as much pleasure in their son taking part in these activities as Dane does himself.

What amazed me about Dane was how after a hard day on the bike (cycling at times more than a hundred kilometers each day) there he would be without fail each night out on the dance floor dancing with everyone in sight. Then, after a night of dancing, he'll nearly always be among the first to awake before dawn to get in the breakfast line and then on the bike for another grueling ride.

Each morning you can hear him chatting away, jogging his memory with all the tasks he has to do before he hits the road. One morning he wanted desperately to ride with his cast of new girlfriends from the ride. He waited patiently for us all to get out of bed and get ready. But he couldn't help himself—the moment we were all on the bikes he sped off and there was no way we were going to catch up! We did, however, manage to stop him dancing long enough that night to get a photograph—Dane with his six new girlfriends . . . .

On a bush walk (during which I struggled to keep up) Dane told me of his planned trip to New Zealand with his girlfriend, his successes in weight-lifting, and that his mother was writing a book. I asked him what she was writing about and he gleefully replied, "Me" . . . .

The mass media in which I work tends to categorize people by their disability and label them accordingly. For example, someone like Dane would be known as a disabled athlete. But for me, he's just a friend who is an absolute delight to be around.

That's what I love about the picture of Dane on my fridge. People see him first as a champion—which indeed he is—rather than someone with autism. And I'm sure in a few years' time, that medal will be an Olympic one.

The weight-lifting Helen Pitt refers to came about as a result of Dane's regular visits to the gym, a part of his life from which he derives much pleasure. It is satisfying for him to know exactly what time he'll arrive at the gym, what equipment he'll use, and that any change in his gym routine will arise from his own achievements. He's always preferred to compete with himself, to achieve a result without the pressures of teamwork. And, of course, the gym's equipment is big!

We couldn't have asked for a finer young man than Jon Tapper to supervise Dane's gym activities. Through our local Interchange, Jon agreed to become a peer support for Dane. He took Dane to the gym's social activities like fishing, barbecues and discos, and they became great friends. The gym allows Dane to interact with others on his own terms. I'm certain he knows more people in the Bega Valley than Rod and I do!

While Rod and I were proud of Dane's athletic prowess, we had never imagined him as a weight-lifter. But a member of the Victoria Drug Free Power Lifting Association (VDFPA) observed him in the gym and suggested he train for competitive power lifting. The three of us went to a competition in Bendigo to see what this was all about, and Dane was seriously impressed. He decided he would enjoy the sport and wanted to compete in the forthcoming Apollo Power Challenge in West Melbourne.

Rod became Dane's official coach and a training regime was established. After months of rigorous training the big day finally arrived, and a fan club of friends came to cheer him on. We were devastated when we discovered Dane's lifting belt didn't meet Apollo Challenge guidelines, but another generous competitor saw our plight and offered Dane the loan of a suitable belt.

At last the competition began. Most competitors nodded gravely as their scores improved, maybe raising a hand to acknowledge a personal best. Dane's face lit up as his scores improved and, with each broad smile, the audience joined his fan club's enthusiastic applause. They recognized his special needs but it was his effort and results that they applauded.

As Dane prepared to top his best score, voices called, "Come on, Smiley! You can do it, Smiley!" The voices quieted as Dane leaned down to grasp the bar. Then there was a roar of delight as he lifted the bar above his head. Dane gently placed the bar on the floor and thrust his hands into the air with the sheer joy of achievement.

An official noted how gently Dane replaced his bar while other competitors dropped theirs to the floor with a crash. I thought Dane was being polite, but he said, "No, it's nothing to do with good manners. It takes real strength to do that!"

Dane was delighted to find his name in the next Apollo newsletter: "Congratulations to first-time lifter Dane Waites, also in the 100 kg class. It's great to see someone really enjoying his lifting. Hope to see you back again in February. Next time we'll have to put a bit more weight on the bar!"

They did put more weight on the bar and in February 1999, a few months before his twenty-fifth birthday, Dane won a trophy!

Friends for life

To celebrate Dane's achievement, Margaret invited us to dinner, and she insisted we go to a particular restaurant. The manager stepped forward as we arrived. She was a tall, elegant young woman with short-cropped hair and a beautiful smile.

"Good evening," she said. "May I help . . . ."

Her eyes widened with pleasure as she recognized Margaret. Then Dane stepped forward, extending his hand and gazing intently at her. She gasped with delight. "Oh, I don't believe this!"

Dane asked, "Jennifer? Is it you, Jennifer?"

It was Jennifer Emery-Smith, the little girl to whom Dane had spoken his very first words at Warrawong Day Care Kindergarten. She wiped tears from her eyes as she turned to greet another group of guests, and I asked Dane if he'd recognized her.

He replied, "No, but I knew her voice. I'll never forget Jennifer's voice, Mum."

Later we talked, and talked! The grown woman willingly answered the questions we'd ached to ask the little girl twenty years ago:

I never once felt sorry for Dane. I don't think I was
aware that he didn't speak. It just didn't matter. When
my father lost the use of his voice some years ago it was
as though Dane had prepared me for this. I've always
had wonderful communication with my father; we talk
in the same way as I talked with Dane. We don't have to
use words to talk. There was no having to explain
anything with Dane. He did nothing to hurt me, in the
way other children do. He made me feel safe and special.

I do remember the day that Dane spoke to me.
I'd not heard him speak before and I knew this was
something different when he said, "Yes, I can." I
remember saying, "What's my name?" and him saying,
"Jenny." To me Dane always could speak, because we
were such good friends. So the importance of my hearing
his voice came and went quickly.

I remembered Dane's fifth birthday when he and Jennifer had sat together at McDonald's. He was withdrawn and without speech, but his devoted little friend stayed by his side. Now here were these same two people talking, reminiscing and laughing together! What a precious gift that evening was for Dane from his loving godmother Margaret.

Later Dane showed me Jennifer's business card. She had written a message on the back: "Take care, Dane! We will be friends for life. Love always, Jennifer."

Another very special friend in Dane's life is Erin Young. Their friendship has blossomed since their days at Irabina, and both families agree that Dane and Erin should be given every possible opportunity to maintain and develop this friendship.

Shared family vacations over the years have allowed this to happen. More recently these vacations took on a new dimension when they went on an escorted group tour of New Zealand with the Assist Travel agency. They had a wonderful time and I know Dane's life will be enriched by organizations such as Assist Travel.

In Erin's words, "We're very independent!"

But it's only the flexibility and practical attitudes of individuals and organizations that respect issues such as Dane's need for daily time out to think aloud that makes this precious independence possible. It is essential for Dane to have this time to think aloud. He understands that this behavior is unacceptable in public and tries to confine it to his own private space. While this presents no problem at home, we must make allowances if he's going to be involved with other people on a vacation or during an event such as the RTA Big Bike Rides.

I cannot explain why it is that Dane thinks aloud so eloquently. His everyday speech tends to be hesitant and toneless, yet his think aloud monologue is articulate and expressive. I do know he thinks aloud to mentally catalog the events and conversations of his day; to clarify changes in his daily routine; and to hurry himself to meet an appointment, or to leave home for work at the appropriate time. At work, if he's not performing a task adequately, he'll think aloud to get back to his list. He really gives himself a scolding—or he gives "Dane," his unseen companion, a scolding.

Dane's developing life skills continue to delight us. He'll take the initiative on occasions such as birthdays and Mother's Day. Without any prompting from us he'll buy an appropriate card and print his own affectionate message inside. In Bega, he can make a purchase in any store, and while he can't formulate an exact payment the staff always offers to help.

It dawned on me slowly after we moved to the Bega Valley that Dane's level of functioning was no longer an issue. What is important now is Dane the individual. I no longer need to organize every moment of his day. Almost imperceptibly, he has begun taking control of his own time and space and while he still needs to know what we'll do next weekend, he'll occupy himself between organized activities. We can occasionally leave him at home alone for a few hours. That's a far cry from the days when we dared not allow him out of our sight.

Nowadays we no longer try to modify his inappropriate behavior. Rather, we support his acceptable behavior by enhancing his quality of life. It has taken me years to properly recognize that the events leading up to inappropriate behavior are more significant than the behavior itself. Instead of waiting in dread for the next outburst, I ask myself if he is feeling calm and happy. If not, then I begin supporting him before the onset of inappropriate behavior.

Dane remains very susceptible to suggestions from others, especially to teasing and joking. He'll respond to remarks or suggestions from a prankster with smiles and it might be days or even weeks before the incident spills over into inappropriate behavior. By then the cause may well be forgotten. His peers cannot be expected to connect today's inappropriate behavior with a three-week-old prank, or to recognize the pain and confusion behind his agreeable smile. They are simply learning now what I learned years ago in doctor's office: that Dane smiles and says "yes" to please other people.

It is most uncommon for a person with autism to recognize other people's expressions and to demonstrate their own feelings through facial expression. As a child Dane had to learn about facial expressions and to interpret their meaning. Now he can read an expression within a second, and this puts him in control. It is extraordinary that not only has he developed this ability to read other people's expressions, he can also respond appropriately and make his own adjustments to a situation. Occasionally, though, he looks to us for confirmation that he's read a face correctly. Is Dad really angry or just pretending? Is Mum joking?

Today Dane is also able to express his feelings verbally. He is quite comfortable saying he loves us. His facial expression and relaxed body language leave us in no doubt that he feels good about expressing his feelings in this way.

Dane has explained to us many of the incidents from his childhood that arose from confused perceptions. Recently I asked if he remembered why he always screamed when we drove along a certain stretch of the road.

He replied, "Yes, I remember. I was scared the cows and the horses would fall off the steep hills." It was as simple as that—cows on steep hillsides. If only I'd understood at the time.

When I asked why he screamed when we drove along the Bulleen Freeway, he replied, "I was scared the clouds were going to break the trees."

I had to think about this for a while, then I recalled how a bank of low clouds often appeared to hover on the horizon, over a grove of trees. I knew how much Dane loved trees and clouds yet in a lifetime of driving that freeway I would never have made this connection.

I asked why he rocked his head from side to side and sang himself to sleep, whether it was a habit.

Without hesitation he replied, "That's how I stop the other sounds, Mum. That's how my mind thinks about sleep." To this day it's not unusual to hear Dane softly singing himself to sleep.

Every sound competes for Dane's attention. He's tuned into every buzz and stir. I'll whisper something and he'll respond from upstairs. Thinking aloud helps overcome these extraneous sounds. When he started thinking aloud very loudly at work, I asked him why he was doing it, and why only sometimes and not all the time.

"It has to be loud, Mum, or I can hear the praying and I can't concentrate on my list."

Praying? What praying?

Then I remembered the small church opposite his workplace. I checked and discovered that the church had introduced a mid-week service some weeks before. Dane was unaccustomed to the distant sounds of prayer and had become confused.

Constantly we are reminded not to assume that Dane always understands what we say. In a self-serve bistro one day, I told him to take only a small serving of food, but he returned to our table with his plate piled high.

"Dane, I asked you to take a small serving," I said. "It's rude to fill your plate like that."

He looked at me, crestfallen. "What's a small serving, Mum? You've never shown me. What does it mean?"

There was so much pain in his voice. We thought he understood the difference between big and small but even after all those years he couldn't relate this understanding to helpings of food. We hadn't explained the difference between a big serving and a small serving. How many other questions remain unanswered?

Misunderstandings can occur in so many ways. Rod and I often see Dane running or riding his bike on our country roads yet he won't pause to greet us. We are lucky to get a fleeting smile or a half-hearted wave. Yet he is always delighted to greet us at the end of his excursion.

We assumed his reluctance to acknowledge us represented his dislike of change. When I was forced recently to interrupt one of his runs to ask him a question, I discovered that this assumption was quite wrong. He answered my question politely, but was clearly displeased at the interruption. At home that evening he asked, "Was that cheating, Mum?"

I asked, "What do you mean, Dane? When did you think you were cheating?"

He replied, "When I stopped running to talk to you. Was that cheating?"

Dane's echolalia is still with us. We use it as a tool to teach him good manners. For example, we suggest that, when meeting someone for the first time, he offers his hand and says, "Good day. My name is Dane. How are you?" He's still most comfortable with given, learned replies but he's also open to suggestions as to how he can vary these replies. Now we're likely to hear Dane's responses and not those of his friends. But we cannot depend on this. We cannot overlook his echolalia.

We were reminded of this one evening when Rod and Dane picked me up from my book group after Dane had finished a workout at the gym. They arrived as we were having supper and I tried to engage him in conversation. "Dane, did you have a good session at the gym?" I asked.

"Yes, Mum."

"How was Jon?"

"Good."

"How was Tom?"

"Good."

I did so want my friends to see that Dane was capable of more than monosyllabic replies. Surely he'd have something to say about Parrot.

So I asked, "And how was Parrot, Dane?"

He flashed me a broad smile. "Oh, Parrot's gone out to hit the booze!"

Fifteen teacups froze in mid-air. The book group ladies were most understanding when we explained Dane had echoed an expression from the gym. Parrot's legendary thirst will forever remind me to avoid open-ended questions in polite company!

The pain and confusion of autism is invisible. Unlike the person with visible scarring or a plaster cast, it is only the characteristic behaviors that denote a person with autism.

It would be easy for a stranger to say of Dane, "What a pleasant young man. He goes to work and drives a car, and yet they say he's autistic! Oh well, he must be getting better then. Surely he's almost cured."

If Dane were to undergo today the same assessments he had when he was six, he would probably not appear as classic autistic. Yet Dane is, and always will be, a person with classic autism. This disability still interferes with what he hears, sees and touches.

However, despite his characteristic "triad of impairments" (in the areas of socialization, communication and imagination), Dane has developed sufficient skills to function as a loved and respected individual. He'll never have the powers of imagination but with so many learning experiences from which to draw, his overall coping mechanisms have improved greatly.

Recently I met Dr. Lorna Wing, the author of *Autistic Children: A Guide for Parents*, the book which had such a great influence on our life. Dr. Wing's first question touched me deeply. "Junee, please tell me. Is Dane happy? Does he have a good life?"

I felt so proud as I told her about Dane and showed her photographs of his happy smile.

Dane has known that we have been writing this book since its inception. He has enjoyed the reminiscences and browsing through albums and scrapbooks. His extraordinary memory for people and places has saved its writers hours of time. His answer when we asked if he understood why we were writing the book was gratifying: "Yes, Mum—to help children with autism, and to help their parents, and to give them hope."

He followed this with a remark that surprised me. He said, "I had autism, didn't I?"

For years Dane hasn't used the word "autism" in relation to himself. It's just too painful. Only in reference to his childhood will he sometimes give autism its name.

Occasionally people ask me if Dane knows that he is "different." Of course he knows! This knowledge tore him apart in his early teens when he questioned his identity and his place in the world. Now he simply accepts that he is a person with special needs. He prefers to leave his autism behind at Irabina. "I had autism." That's the key to Dane's self-image.

Rod and I have no wish to debate the issues of autism with our son. Why should we impose the cold, stark reality: *There is no cure for autism!* His silence, his acute echolalia, his childhood behavior can be left behind but not the autism. Autism is a pervasive developmental disorder.

I believe we have helped our son to live in our world, and to be happy. That's all we ever really wanted for him. Just to be happy. And yet despite our best efforts we cannot even take this for granted. Just making sense of his surroundings and our confusing social expectations will always be confronting him.

From time to time he still says, "It's so hard, Mum. It's so hard."

Afterword

When I first heard the words "pervasive development disorder" I experienced emotional turmoil. The impact of these words overwhelmed me. I felt challenged to acknowledge and respond, but I did not know how.

I can appreciate why many parents prefer the term "autistic spectrum disorder"—it sounds less threatening.

As my awareness of the nature of autism emerged, so too did my understanding of the word "pervasive." Autism is not just a segment of a person we can ignore or remove. It *is* pervasive. It *is* a way of being. Given this realization and the gradual ability to work with, rather than against, autism, so too did hope become a reality.

Only by relinquishing my early expectations, and opening up in an endeavor to comprehend the world of autism, have I learned not to grieve for my son who never was. Rather, I give thanks for the remarkable young man who is my son.

Glossary

Asperger syndrome: Severe and sustained social impairments, but not as severe in the communication area. The impairments seem more subtle in the very young child, but become more apparent as the child reaches pre-school and school age. The Asperger child/adult is usually in the normal intelligence range.

References: Wing, L., *The Autistic Spectrum*, Ulysses Press, 2001, and *DSM-IV-TR*, American Psychiatric Society, 2001.

autism: A triad of impairments, in relation to social awareness, communication and imagination. The word "autism" is derived from the Greek *autos*, meaning "self" or "alone."

being the wind: Dane repeatedly flapped found objects in order to "be the wind."

circles concept: A series of concentric circles relating to personal space beginning with self as the center.

echolalia: Constant repetition of words and phrases, possibly without meaning to the speaker.

flapping: This refers to Dane's compulsive and repetitive movement of found objects, usually a leaf or scrap of paper.

hang-ups: Refers to found objects (e.g. string or threads) stretched between solid objects to create straight lines.

social story: A simple, clearly printed single page story (in Dane's instance), offering an effective visual communication technique.

straight lines: Dane's childhood obsession with arrangements of toys and Legos pieces etc., fence lines, mortar lines and two given points joined by taut threads (hang-ups).

thinking aloud: monologue or "self-talk" used by Dane to overwhelm other sounds, thus allowing his thought processes to function.

Autism resources

ARCH National Respite Network and Resource Center
www.chtop.com/locator.htm

Asperger Syndrome Coalition of the United States, Inc. (ASC–US)
www.asperger.org

Autism Resources
Includes an extensive listing of books relevant to autism
www.autism-resources.com

Autism Society of America (ASA)
www.autism-society.org

Birth to Three
State-by-state contact information for programs for children under age three
www.birth23.org/Programs/OtherStates.asp

Cure Autism Now (CAN)
www.canfoundation.org

National Alliance for Autism Research (NAAR)
> www.naar.org

National Information Center for Children and Youth with Handicaps
> Offers legal information
> www.nichcy.org

National Organization of Mental Retardation (ARC)
www.thearc.org

O.A.S.I.S. (Online Asperger Syndrome Information and Support)
> www.udel.edu/bkirby/asperger

Yale Child Study Center—Developmental Disabilities Clinic and Research Home Page
> www.autism.fm

Addresses of local autistic societies can be obtained from the Autism Society of America (ASA) headquarters in Maryland or from their website.

Autism Society of America
> 7910 Woodmont Avenue, Suite 300
> Bethesda, MD 20814-3067
> Phone: 301-657-0881 or 800-3AUTISM
> Fax: 301-657-0869
> www.autism-society.org
> info@autism-society.org

Index

Acknowledgements

This book belongs to Dane. We only needed to write the story.

First, our most profound thanks and gratitude must go to Margaret Whitcombe SJC for her unconditional love and commitment within her role as godmother, and friend. *Love and peace, Margaret.*

Our sincere thanks for giving Dane an appreciation of family connections goes to Norman Oakley (dec.), Alice (dec.) and Jack (O'pa) Wuillemin, Maxine, Louis and Andrea (dec.) Wuillemin and their respective families; Dianne and Jhon Casey and Aaron, Dion and Joel (dec.) Casey; Seona and Mardi Kennedy and Maree Ranicar.

Many thanks are due to a variety of wonderful people, all of whom have helped in creating and enriching Dane's remarkable life, and who have checked relevant facts contained in this book.

Toni and Michael O'Sullivan for enduring friendship; Llewyn, Greer and Kiely-Lynn Waters for lifelong friendship and our introduction to the Bega Valley; Pam and Norman Bull and family for never forgetting Dane's birthday and Jim (dec.), Kay, Gavin, Tanya and Scott Dimitri, for their empathetic friendship.

Dr. Lorna Wing for her book *Autistic Children*—an answer to our prayers—and Patricia Leevers for her astute recommendation that Junee and Rod read *Autistic Children*.

Kath and Geoff Nicholls for welcoming Dane into their home on so many occasions. Erin Young for love of Dane as a special friend, and Diane, Clarrie and Kendrah Young for shared holidays and the photographs to recall the many happy experiences.

For dedicated and creative teaching from the heart: Jean Hayward, Joan Groube, Nell Jones, Shelley Reinholdt, Margaret Smith, Kevin Hogg and Olga Hintze.

For prayers and support and for becoming Dane's second family, the Sisters of St. Joseph of Cluny, especially the Kew (Australia) and Paris (France) Communities. For prayers and encouragement: the Poor Clare Nuns at Campbelltown, especially Sr. Clare Donnegan and Sr. Collette Jones, and in Papua New Guinea, especially Sr. Eblina Peters.

Owen Awcock OFM, Peter Cantwell OFM and Brian Gallagher MSC for mentorship in our journey of faith. Eleanor Davis for thoughtful and meaningful preparation for Dane's Holy Communion.

Dane's godfather for all seasons, William Gayfer, and Walter and Lyn Kane for kindness and support—especially during our ordeal in the Allergy Unit.

Elizabeth Gower for loyal friendship and sharing the joy and sorrow, and for understanding and interpreting Dane's echolalia.

To Caterina Gentile and her warm and welcoming family—*mille grazie!* Vicki and Michael Colgrave, and Tom, Annie and Toby Colegrave for the peace of the *Luminarius*, and for sharing with Dane the joys of Stringybark Farm. For friendship, fun, speech camps and support groups, Liz and Roy Wilks, and Duane, Miles and Amy Wilks.

Joan Murphy-Clair, whose help made airline travel a joyful reality for Dane. In Fiji—Ann and Bob Harness and family, and Lewis Whitcombe—*vinaka vakalevu!* Sam and Jen Ginsberg—*shalom.* Susan McKoy for becoming a vital link in our circle of supportive friendship.

Vicki Bitsika, our incalculable thanks for help in so many aspects of our lives during Dane's difficult teenage years, and for the courage to develop a new approach in counseling and befriending Dane.

Professor Bruce J. Tonge for recognizing the role of parents as co-therapists, and encouraging Dane to develop his full potential.

Kaye and David Francis for friendship during and after Churinga, and for sharing with us the serenity of Cathedral Mountain. Marg Evans, for introducing Dane to music at Irabina and later, for introducing us to Anja Tait. Anja Tait, for introducing Dane to a new world of culture and expression, through their mutual love of music. *Peace always, Anja.* Margaret Uren for sharing her love of poetry and rhythmic language with Dane. *A huge bunch of sun-flowers, Margaret.*

Dr. Carl L Parsons for perceptive appraisal of Dane's language, Dane's introduction to the world of computers and the expansion of his communication skills. Shelley O'Connell for creative input into preparing Dane for his first work experience at the Burwood "Caf."

Lorna Harman, Diane Kennedy, Doreen Smith and Elaine Page who came into Dane's life to offer respite care, and gave us so much more than this.

Ray and Cheryl Ryan and family for friendship and support during our move to Bega, and especially Ray for always "being there" for Dane, with his sports. Beth and Gordon Hudson and family for being such great neighbors.

Geraldine Taylor and Mario Mazoni for helping Dane achieve his dream of obtaining his driver's license, and our neighbors Pat and Bruce Durrant for support and encouragement in this and all of Dane's recent achievements.

Jon Tapper, whose ongoing friendship and support has meant so much to Dane. For expanding Dane's love of bike riding and opening doors to new friendships and experiences—Kym Mogridge, Mary Hourigan Mullens, David Mullens and Helen Pitt.

Virginia Fitzclarence for friendship, and an ongoing professional and tenacious approach in supporting Dane in open employment. Leo and Antonio Papalia, proprietors of Bega Valley Motors and Dane's employers for six years, for whom it was surely and act of courage to accept his inconsistent behavior; and Leigh Hardingham for friendship and support for Dane in their workplace. Samantha French of the Department of Family and Community Services whose efforts on Dane's behalf resulted in his becoming one of the first employees to join the NSW Government's Supported Wage Scheme.

Dr. Michael A Lawless, in accepting Dane (for Lasik surgery) as his first patient with special needs.

Ros Langford of Assist Travel for opening the way for Dane to travel independently, with appropriate assistance.

Jennifer Emery-Smith for renewing friendship with Dane after so many years, and for sharing her unique insights into their early childhood—*friends for life.*

For invaluable assistance in researching this book: Margaret Whitcombe; Pat Jones (ex Respite Care Bega Valley Inc.); Neiliya Arnolda, Lydian Wheen of Warrawong Day Care Kindergarten; Judy Thomson and the Association of Graduates in Early Childhood Studies; Neerosh Mudaly, Jane Watson Brown (Librarian) of the Spastic Society of Victoria; Richard Plum and Andrea Timms and Speech Patholology Australia; Pamela Ralphs; Kate Gilchrist and Anita Pollard of the NSW Arts Law Society; Dianne Bailey-Tribe and Autism Services Irabina Early Intervention Program for Children with Autism Spectrum Disorder; Imelda Dodds and the Autistic

Association of NSW; Amanda Golding and Autism Victoria; Rose Clark and Autism Tasmania.

For practical support during the preparation of this book: Marie Swinbourne, Michelle Buckley, Roslyn Leslie, Kathleen Boyne, Sean Knight, Sue Brierty, Margaret Nolan, Bob Counahan, Phil McKendry, Margaret Trowbridge, Jennifer A. Williams, Margaret Taylor and Sue Wallace.

Stuart Carless for his fantastic photographs.

Gabriel Farago and Tom Ligeti for their valuable appraisal of the draft manuscript, and encouragement and ongoing support in Dane's journey.

Judith Winters for encouragement and valuable editorial input; the Fellowship of Australia Writers (Far South Coast Regional) for support; also Maggie Benjamin and Camp Creative and especially Patricia Gaut for innovative tutoring.

HarperCollins Publishers for kind permission to reprint Fr. Brian Gallagher's poem "Damian" from *People's Prayer* and the *Herald* and *Weekly Times* and John Casamento for kind permission to reprint the photograph from *The Sun News Pictorial*, 15 April 1976.

Our agent Mary Cunnane for enthusiasm, keen insight and belief in the importance of this book. Shona Martyn at HarperCollins Publishers for her early interest, Cathy Jenkins at HarperCollins Publishers for intelligent guidance and Jane Bowring for insightful copyediting. Sarah Gentle and Susannah Burgess at HarperCollins Publishers.

There are so many other wonderful people who are special to this story. For your friendship, your help and your love—we thank you. God bless you all.

Other books by Ulysses Press/Seastone

ANXIETY AND DEPRESSION: A NATURAL APPROACH
2nd edition, Shirley Trickett, $10.95

While traditional medicine focuses on alleviating isolated symptoms, this book relates to you as a whole person, offering an effective treatment program.

THE AUTISTIC SPECTRUM: A PARENTS' GUIDE TO UNDERSTANDING AND HELPING YOUR CHILD
Lorna Wing, M.D., $14.95

Incorporating the latest developments in this ever-changing area, *The Autistic Spectrum* clearly and simply explains how to better understand your child's specific condition.

HOW MEDITATION HEALS: A SCIENTIFIC EXPLANATION
Eric Harrison, $12.95

In straightforward, practical terms, *How Meditation Heals* reveals how and why meditation improves the natural functioning of he human body.

HOW TO MEDITATE: AN ILLUSTRATED GUIDE TO CALMING THE MIND AND RELAXING THE BODY
Paul Roland, $16.95

Offers a friendly approach to calming the mind and raising consciousness through various techniques, including meditation, visualization, body scanning for tension and mantras.

KNOW YOUR BODY: THE ATLAS OF ANATOMY
2nd edition, Introduction by Emmet B. Keeffe, M.D., $14.95

Provides a comprehensive, full-color guide to the human body.

MIGRAINES: A NATURAL APPROACH
2nd edition, Sue Dyson, $12.95

Shows how to take effective action and details strategies for managing this distressing problem.

101 SIMPLE WAYS TO MAKE YOUR HOME & FAMILY SAFE
IN A TOXIC WORLD
Beth Ann Petro Roybal, $11.95

Sheds light on common toxins found around the house and offers parents straightforward ways to protect themselves and their children.

PILATES WORKBOOK: ILLUSTRATED STEP-BY-STEP GUIDE
TO MATWORK TECHNIQUES
Michael King, $12.95

Illustrates the core matwork movements exactly as Joseph Pilates intended them to be performed; readers learn each movement by following the photographic sequences and explanatory captions.

SIMPLY RELAX: AN ILLUSTRATED GUIDE
TO SLOWING DOWN AND ENJOYING LIFE
Dr. Sarah Brewer, $15.95

In a beautifully illustrated format, this book clearly presents physical and mental disciplines that show readers how to relax.

WHAT WOULD BUDDHA DO?:
101 ANSWERS TO LIFE'S DAILY DILEMMAS
Franz Metcalf, $9.95

Much as the "WWJD?" books help Christians live better lives by drawing on the wisdom of Jesus, this "WWBD?" book provides advice on improving your life by following the wisdom of another great teacher—Buddha.

YOU DON'T HAVE TO SIT ON THE FLOOR:
MAKING BUDDHISM PART OF YOUR EVERYDAY LIFE
Jim Pym, $12.95

Explains how to make Buddhism part of your life while being true to the customs and beliefs you have always followed.

To order these books call 800-377-2542 or 510-601-8301, fax 510-601-8307, e-mail ulysses@ulyssespress.com, or write to Ulysses Press, P.O. Box 3440, Berkeley, CA 94703. All retail orders are shipped free of charge. California residents must include sales tax. Allow two to three weeks for delivery.

About the authors

Junee Waites lives in Bega with her husband Rod and her son Dane. She has worked tirelessly to promote the rights of people with autistic spectrum disorders. **Helen Swinbourne** is a journalist, photographer and writer.